Life Path by Design

*Coach Yourself to
Your Own Charmed Life*

Linda Drevenstedt

Life Path by Design

By Linda Drevenstedt

Copyright © 2016 by Linda Drevenstedt

Cover Design by Colleen Davis

All rights reserved. No part of this publication may be reproduced, distributed, or transmitted in any form or by any means, including photocopying, recording, or other electronic or mechanical methods, or by any information storage and retrieval system, without the prior written permission of the publisher and author, except in the case of brief quotations embodied in critical reviews and certain other non-commercial uses permitted by copyright law.

ISBN: 978-1-944177-23-2 (p)
ISBN: 978-1-944177-24-9 (e)

Crescendo Publishing, LLC
300 Carlsbad Village Drive
Ste. 108A, #443
Carlsbad, California 92008-2999

www.CrescendoPublishing.com
GetPublished@CrescendoPublishing.com

A Message from the Author

https://youtu.be/hcygNI2P9iw

To help you get the most out of my book, I have provided some complimentary bonus material that will help lead you to your own charmed life.

You can download all of these items at:

http://www.lifepathbydesign.net/

People Love Life Path by Design

"Oh, did I need your book about 30 years ago. Your book would have lead me to my strengths not my weaknesses. What a wonderful gift and a "must read" to anyone who is still questioning "their worth" "their direction" and how to achieve "the charmed life."

~Ginger Carey Doherty

"I have known and worked with Linda Drevenstedt for over 25 years. During that time she has brought the best out of life and this book is a perfect example of that attitude. Her research is impeccable and creates a wonderful sense of belief to the reader."

~David M. Reznik, DDS

"Linda Drevenstedt is one canny woman who knows how to navigate the pitfalls that we encounter as we strike out for new personal and professional goals and adventures in our life. The power and joy of her book is that she makes what can seem like overwhelming changes do-able step by step and provides the resources that allow the reader to find their own power and effectiveness in their own, unique way. This book is not only a brilliant road map but also an extremely useful resource guide. Keep it handy. You'll want to refer to it often!"

~Bill Lamond, author of BORN TO LEAD.

"To be a great leader, the major trait you need is to, "know thyself." Life Path By Design is an excellent book which enables the reader to fully understand that we all can have a "Charmed Life." Linda's developed guidance to find "your Charmed Life" and challenges us to examine our purpose and principles and she passes this thought process on to others which is invaluable. This book is full of processes and steps to help grow your courage and insight into building the life you always wanted."

~Hugh Doherty, DDS, CFP, CEO, Business of Dental Practice LLC

"Linda Drevenstedt is that fresh voice in self-motivation that many of us have been seeking. Her insights in Life Path by Design *bring practical observations to the process of change. I am so glad to see someone combining the no-nonsense applications of coaching in the business world with the spiritual truths which speaks to our soul's growth. Linda's book is a delight to read. She has a genius of making complicated concepts easy to understand. This is one of the first books I recommend to people who are truly ready to make big changes in their lives."*

~Ken Wilcox, Senior Minister Center for Spiritual Leading St Augustine, FL

Table of Contents

Welcome 1

Chapter 1
Who is this person designing a new life path? 5

Chapter 2
Whose path are you walking? 15

Chapter 3
Where do you want the path to go? 39

Chapter 4
What stones are in your path? 67

Chapter 5
Why are there twists and turns in my path? 79

Chapter 6
What is this pain telling you? 89

Chapter 7
Can you handle life's dementors? 97

Chapter 8
Are you ready to walk an unknown path? 123

Chapter 9
Is it time for a walk? 135

Chapter 10
Do you have the energy you need for your
life path? 147

Chapter 11
How do you relate to your partner along your evolving life path?..155

Chapter 12
Who ya gonna call?...165

ETC. – Epilogue..177

In Appreciation...179

About Linda Drevenstedt "Cultivating Potential in People" 181

Connect with Linda 183

Resources for Life Path by Design 185

Welcome

What do you mean, a charmed life?

    What would a charmed life be like for you? How would you design your own charmed life? These questions begin your quest. You see, most people look at their life and see what they do *not* want. They complain about their job, their boss, their coworkers, their partner, their parents, their children, and blah, blah and blah. Here in the good ole US of A, we often define our life by the problems, the complaints, and the drama.

    There are others who live in the conversation called "Someday I'll ...." These are fuzzy dreamers who talk about what they are going to do ... when they win the lottery. ...when their ship comes in. ...when they inherit the big bucks ... when they are older ... when they live in a different place. That's sad though. They may never purchase the lottery ticket, and they have not put a ship out to sea.

Then again, maybe you are just OK. You are humming along satisfied, not really going for anything better in life. Put this book down. It is not for you.

Maybe you want more out of life but, but, but ....

What do you really want? A more fulfilling career? More passion in your vocation? Would you like to travel to foreign lands or to live at the beach? Would you like a new home? Would you like a better-paying job? Would you like an intimate, fun relationship with your significant other? Would you like to have your children shape up? Would you like to get along better with your parents or siblings? Would you like to be fitter, to eat better, or to have more "me" time?

The truth is this: you can design your own charmed life.

> "If it is to be, it is up to me."
>
> William Johnsen

You can coach yourself to design and live a life that is charmed. As you ponder the question "How would I define a charmed life?" you may want to take time to journal or meditate on it. I have provided you with a link to a meditation on my website to help you with the process of defining your charmed life.

www.lifepathbydesign.net

Allow yourself to desire

The root of the word "de-sire" is "of the father." Depending on your faith, picture God as you define him/her being a partner with you in creating a charmed life. Our old conditioning often gets in the way of our charmed life. There are a lot of people, experiences, and events rattling around in your mind, steering you in a direction of "their" choice. This book contains exercises, meditations, worksheets, and links to assist you in coaching yourself. You will coach yourself, back to yourself and your desired life.

For now, just allow the vision of YOUR charmed life to occupy more of your thoughts. If fact, if you will spend just five minutes a day gaining clarity in the mental picture of your charmed life, you will move closer and closer to it.

What would it **BE** like to live a charmed life? What would it **FEEL** like to live your charmed life? What would you **DO** in this charmed life? What would you **HAVE** in your charmed life? **WHO** would you be with in your charmed life? **WHERE** would you live in your charmed life? You can define all of this, especially how it will feel. Your feelings are strong motivators. Allow yourself to take time to bathe in the charmed life as you see it.

Keep it under your hat

You don't have to announce anything or share anything with anyone else at this point. This is your own personal life path design process. On your own, you will coach yourself through the exercises, going at your own pace. Life Path by Design is an inside job. Nobody "out there" needs to change. In this Life Path by Design process, "me, myself, and I" get to do the work of designing a charmed life path.

Oh no, there is the word "work." Don't skittle away too quickly. Work is always a relative term. If you knew you could work a bit on your own internal processing system to reprogram your life and move steps or leaps closer to a charmed life, would it be worth it to spend a bit of time on some "work"?

Chapter by chapter, process by process, meditation by meditation, you will whittle away at the barriers to designing your life path, your own charmed life. For now, spend time with the vision of what your charmed life would be like. Your design will be different from mine or anyone else's. That is one of the great things about taking the first step on the path to designing your own life path. You will see how to get into the driver's seat of life.

Welcome to the journey of your personal growth and your charmed life path.

> "We grow to the degree we want to grow. It is the depth from which we want this growth that makes it begin to take place."
>
> Swami Chetanananda

Chapter 1

Who is this person designing a new life path?

Chapter 1

Who is this person designing a new life path?

What are your strengths? What are your values? Answering these two questions builds the foundation for designing the life you want to lead. Your life path will be easier to design when you understand your own strengths and values. If you are in a job or relationships where you are not allowed to express or use your own strengths and you are not able to express your own values, then you will not feel charmed. If fact, you can become miserable, depressed, and apathetic and may not even know why.

Taking back your own life path design takes time—time you invest to do a bit of research, meditate, journal, and participate in several exercises. Yes, this is part of the work I mentioned earlier.

Finding Strengths

Behavior or personality strengths provide a firm foundation for defining the environment where you will find the fulfillment you desire in your charmed life. Let me share a quick story of how this played out in my life. Like a lot of women who grew up in the Ozzie and Harriet '50s, I thought nabbing a good husband was all I needed to have a charmed life and live happily ever after. Fast-forward fifteen years into the marriage and I knew something was not charmed about my life.

Using the DiSC® profile system, I took one profile with a focus on my role in my marriage. I took another profile without a focus; I responded without using a role definition. WOW! There it was on those two profiles. There in my research, I saw that I was aberrating myself to fit the role of "The Good Little Wife." GOSH, how we can deny our own soul to get along and go along. My fears, old conditioning, and old expectations kept me in the marriage for another five years while I found my way back to myself, discovered my strengths and my values, and began to redesign my life path.

You, too, may have accepted a role expected of you from parents, from your peers, or from your culture, or you may have just fallen into a role without much thought. Maybe you just got a job to pay the bills. Maybe you went into a profession because there was a family history in that profession. Maybe someone told you that you would be good at a particular job. However you got where you are, now is the time to really look at the fit for you.

Behavior Strengths

Initially, start by taking time to discover your strengths by using a behavior/personality assessment; there are many available. The one I have taught for years in my coaching and consulting practice is the DiSC® model. Here is an overview of the DiSC® model to start your research.

In medieval times philosophers divided people into four types, depending on the person's dominant body humor or temperament. The belief was that a dominant humor influenced a person's disposition. A person was sanguine, melancholy, phlegmatic, or choleric. Those terms have long since faded, and today you might hear the terms "Driver" or "Director," "Expressive" or "Influencing," "Amiable" or "Steadiness," and "Conscientious" or "Analytical." There are four main personality or behavior styles in the DiSC® model used in this book. Everyone is capable of behaving in any of the four styles; however, most people are more comfortable in one or two styles. That place of comfort is your area of strength.

The DiSC® four-style model was developed Dr. John Geier and Wiley Publishing, Inc. Our behaviors are an expression of a dominant need. Each behavior style has both strengths and areas for development. There are two broad divisions of behavior and then two subsets of each division, which give four distinct styles or patterns. The two broad categories are Outgoing and

Reserved. The subset of the Outgoing styles includes a style that prefers to interact with people and the other pattern of people who prefer tasks. The subset of the Reserved style includes styles that are Task Oriented and styles that are People Oriented. All four patterns have an important place in the world. There is no one style or pattern that is better than another, just different. The following DiSC ® model shows you the four styles.

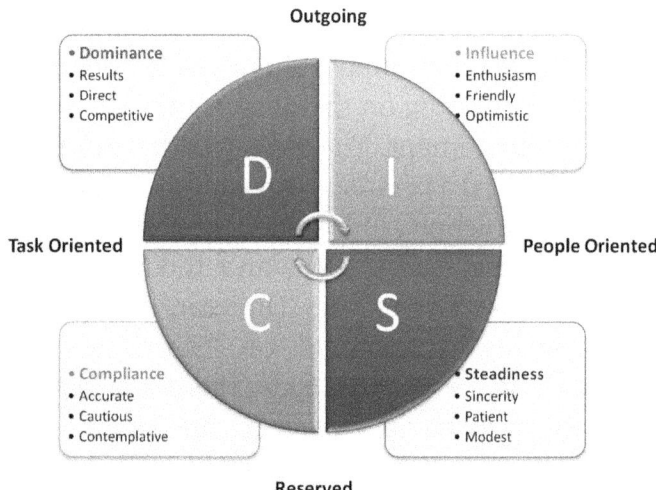

©Wiley Publishing, Inc.

Dominant, "D" Style Strengths: This Outgoing style includes people who exhibit a need to get results, both from themselves and others. People whose style is Dominant, "D," are task oriented; they are directors who prefer leading the group. Those with "D" as a strength tend to be direct and brief in their communication, impatient about time, and like varied activity. "D" style people like competition and enjoy careers that challenge them such as sales, management, business ownership, military, law, or business development. The bottom line is if "D" is your strength, look to a career path that allows you to be in a leadership role, to manage others, or to work where you can set your own pace and goals.

Influencing, style strengths: The other Outgoing style is the "i" or the Influencing style. People with Influencing as a strength are energized by working with people, exhibit optimism, and are very social. "They never meet a stranger" was a statement made for this style. People of the Influencing style generate enthusiasm for their causes or ideas, tend to be restless when not working with people, and act and respond spontaneously. The "i" strength is persuasion. People who are the "i" style can use their strength in sales, entertainment, personal development, interior decorating, marketing, advertising, customer service, or public relations.

Steadiness, "S" style strengths: The Steadiness style combines Reserved and People Orientation. "S" style strengths include being systematic about their work, genuinely friendly, accepting of others, reliable, and pleasant. If this is your behavior strength, you will want to look for steady, secure situations at work and home. Other "S" style strengths are excellent listening skills, friendliness, and loyalty to job and family. Your life path could enjoy careers in teaching, counseling, health care (such as dental assisting or nursing), as well as other service professions. Of all the behaviors, the

"S" style most wants to balance career and work. They like to keep traditions alive and stay close to family.

Conscientious, "C" style strengths: The second Reserved style has task quality and accuracy as needs. If Conscientious is your behavior strength, your career or vocation strength is the need for quality over quantity in your work. The "C" pattern will be conservative, professional, and formal in communicating. The careers that "C" strength people might choose are accounting, engineering, pharmacy, computer programming, research science, and medicine and dentistry.

Each style is unique and adds variety to our world. There is no one best style. However, in your research, finding a vocation or career path that allows your strengths to unfold and grow will help you have a charmed life by understanding the environment that best fits your behavior style. The more you study the depths of your own behavior style, the more you can understand yourself and then better understand others in your life.

Sidebar: Should you want to take the DiSC® profile online, here is the link to my website. Once you take the profile, I offer a thirty-minute complimentary debrief of your results. www.lifepathbydesign.net

Defining Your Values

Why do you need to define your values? Your values and your behavior style strength are two of the strongest drivers in your life. When you understand yourself through your values and personality/behavior strengths, you are able to build a foundation that assists you in making life choices and designing your life path. If you are in a relationship with a significant other or you are in a workplace where you are in a values conflict, you will not be living a charmed life.

Here is your research project. There is a *Values Sort* available to you on my website: www.lifepathbydesign.net. There are no right or wrong values, just different values for different people. Through my coaching experience, I find that values conflicts are strong stressors in the workplace and in the home. Your Life Path by Design research needs this essential piece of information so that you can clearly define your charmed life future.

Go online now to download your copy of the *Values Sort*. www.lifepathbydeisgn.net. I make it available as a download because this process is valuable to experience as a couple.

One other assessment that I have recently experienced is the Enneagram, another old system of looking at behavior strengths and needs. The more you have in your life path research folder at this point, the better. Here is the link to take a free Enneagram. www.enneagraminstitute.com/rheti-sampler

Using Your Research

Once you can see yourself in the light of both your personality or behavior style and your values, you have a working map to design your charmed life. You can journal or meditate on the kind of environment that you want for your charmed life. Here I am not talking of environment as the beach, the mountains, or the city, but your life environment, which includes the people you share life with and the place and people that you want in your vocation or career.

When my children were little, I wanted to be both a dental hygienist and a mom. I wanted to work only three days per week to fulfill my value of a strong family life and my value of being productive. I also valued an environment of a progressive dental practice where I could be a leader. I interviewed and worked as a temporary hygienist until I found the best dental practice for me. I interviewed the dentist to ensure my values would match up. This was one of the first times I realized my charmed life. My boss said this to me, "You went to dental hygiene school. I did not. Help me make this a state-of-the art practice in the dental hygiene department." It was music to my ears. I worked with my heart and soul to do just that and loved that job and that dental practice for many years.

Your life path design can take you where you want to go. You just need to know what environment allows you to feel like you are leading a charmed life. You will learn to look until you find the job or career that fits who you are, rather than trying to shoehorn yourself into someone else's idea of who or what you should be.

www.lifepathbydeisgn.net

Chapter 2

Whose path are you walking?

Chapter 2

Whose path are you walking?

Your charmed life evolves as you design your own life. Knowing whose life you have been leading can help you find your own path. In this chapter, you'll look at who and what influenced who you are now.

Do you have a Mini-me or two?

Picture a set of Russian stacking dolls. The painted, lacquered sets contain dolls of diminishing size. My set that I got in St. Petersburg, Russia, has five dolls. Each doll has a unique scene painted and then lacquered on it so that it is bright and beautiful. The inside tiniest doll is only one and a half inches tall. Now, picture that tiny doll as your Mini-me, and each of the other dolls as other Mini-mes that you keep protected and hidden. The big outside doll nests all the little ones inside; all the Mini-mes are underneath this shellacked exterior doll. On my shelf, I see only the larger outside nesting doll. In life, we keep our Mini-mes hidden, yet they are there "pulling our strings."

During your life, your Mini-mes develop. You can call it subconscious mind or ego self, but I like Mini-me because each one is a smaller version of you. Your current adult self is now willing to design your own life. However, as you begin to change or develop, you bump into your Mini-mes. This little ego, Mini-me, may be stuck or hardened like the lacquer on the dolls. We toughen up or weaken, and then another life event occurs and we bury the last one and cover over it with the new one. Soon there are several Mini-mes just under the surface that are in control of our experiences, our behaviors, and our very life path.

Uncover your Mini-me(s)

The following outline is your guide for your meditation and journaling. There are some predictable life stages to work with for this exploration and inquiry into your Mini-me self. I suggest that you set aside at least thirty minutes to an hour for each of these stages.

For the meditation, find a quiet, comfortable spot to sit where you will not be disturbed. Sit in a comfortable chair and have your journal and a pen nearby so that as you meditate you will not have to go find these things. I will walk you through the meditation. You can read it over and then meditate on what you have read, or you can record your own voice speaking the meditation. You may also choose to go to my website to find my recording of these meditations. www.lifepathbydesign.net

Meditation on early-life childhood:

Close your eyes and take several very deep, slow breaths. Let whatever you were doing before you sat down melt away. Plant your feet firmly on the floor and take everything off your lap. Take another deep breath, pulling air into your belly, making it extend in a Buddha belly breath. On the next breath, pull air way into your lungs, feel them expand with oxygen, then let this breath out slowly. Now just let your breathing settle in as you relax. Picture yourself at the top of a staircase with ten steps down. As you take a step, hold the handrail that is there, and take a deep breath. Picture yourself becoming younger and younger with each step down until at the last step you are age zero to three. Take a moment to allow your young self to speak to you. Ask this young you these questions:

1. Is there something that you decided about life at this young age? Take a deep breath and feel the answer come. Was there an incident that imprinted upon your younger self? If there is an incident, play it in your mind as a movie and watch all the characters. As you watch the incident play out, be the child. Feel what she feels, what she experiences, and how she comes to a decision about life in that moment. Now, change your role to someone else in the

scene. Pretend or play the role of the father, the mother, the other caretaker in this scene. What is going on in their heart and mind at this time? Look at the whole scene to see how you made a life decision during this time. Feel the feeling of younger you. Breathe several times.

Now, picture yourself at your present age. Take a moment to kneel down and ask this child what she needs to heal, forgive, and be free of this incident and its attached decision. Ask her if she has decided to mistrust others. Did she decide to feel shame? Did she decide to become a tough cookie to meet life and people head-on? Did she decide to feel inferior or unlovable? Did she decide to shrink away and not be seen? Did she decide to fight back? Did she decide to feel guilty about herself and her behavior? Did she decide that the people in her world were to be trusted or not to be trusted? Did she decide to be sickly to get attention or to be a victim of the situation? Does she feel helpless, as if she has no choice because she is so young? Let her talk to you for a moment. Breathe.

Find out what she decided about life at this young age. She took the world as she saw it at this young age and set about to be or do what was required of her to survive and grow. Now, tell her that you are going to take care of her now and give her what see needs to feel safe, secure, and loved just as she is, unconditionally.

Take a moment to be with her and hug her and let her know you are there for her now and forever. You become the parent to your own inner child. Only you know what she really needs to feel loved unconditionally. Take a deep breath and feel the love you have for this young child. Hold her hand as you walk toward the stairs. Kiss her and tell her you will always be close by if she needs you.

Take a breath and begin to walk up the ten stairs. Take a deep breath at each stair until you reach the top. Take one more deep breath and return to the room. Spend a few minutes journaling about what you learned from your younger self.

2. The next part you will do with your journal. This completion process is from Bill Lamond, and it is, as Bill says, like deleting software from your computer. The deletion allows space for a new software program. You can use this process in many places in this book. It is one of your coaching tools to grow yourself along your life path. At each life stage, when you discover a Mini-me that no longer serves you, use the Completion Process that follows.

Completion Process by Bill Lamond

Pick an issue, incident, or situation to use, something about which you want to gain a sense of wholeness because you're feeling diminished. Let's say you're disappointed in yourself because this morning you lost your cool and spoke harshly to your spouse. Think about the familiar computer metaphors "delete" and "save" to direct your action at each step. When you "delete" the item from your mind and move it to your trash can, you create a mental image of getting rid of things you don't need any longer. It opens room for your wholeness.

1. Say what was valuable or gave you pleasure about this subject. (Save)

I spoke my mind, and now he knows exactly how I feel about that. It's out in the open. I was honest about my feelings.

2. Say what was not valuable and didn't give you any pleasure. (Delete)

I hurt his feelings. He left the house in a huff and slammed the door.

3. Apologize for anything you need to apologize for regarding this subject. (Delete)

I called and apologized to him at work. Now I forgive myself for losing control of my emotions.

4. Offer thanks to God (whoever is your higher power source), yourself, and anyone else whom you need to thank regarding this subject. (Delete)

I thank God for her understanding and forgiveness. I thank myself for being wise enough and courageous enough to redeem the relationship.

5. Say anything else that you need to say to be complete with this subject.

(Delete)

This can help me be aware of my triggers so that maybe next time I will catch myself before I verbalize in anger. I am capable of correcting my mistakes.

6. Declare that you are complete, meaning you have said and acknowledged everything that was important about this subject.

This mess is over now. We've both put it behind us. I am whole, complete, and worthy.

7. MOVE ON! Do not dwell on this subject.

Let this seven-step process guide you to a consciousness of joyful completeness.

After you have done a completion process, you will have updated your consciousness, which is not very different from balancing your checkbook or cleaning out a closet. You will be left with a packet of pleasurable information with which to nourish yourself over and over. You will have also deleted all the rest of the information that was taking up room in your consciousness.

WOW, what a feeling to complete this and clean it out of your mental filing cabinet. Take other periods in your life outlined here. Take time for the process to settle in. The Mini-me's decisions have been in the control tower of your life, and you have been at the mercy of their three-, nine-, eleven-, or sixteen-year-old's decisions. What I have found is that the process can leave me almost lightheaded. It is like having a massage—that warm, yummy feeling of being in love with life.

You do not lose forty pounds in an hour (unless you have tummy by-pass surgery), and you will not settle all the Mini-mes in one session. They have been there a long time and have been in control. Just like an unruly child, they may go kicking and screaming, but if you stick to your plan to take your own life back into your hands, it will be worth the journey. You will feel a sense of relief at times and a new sense of emotional power that has been hidden under all of those lacquered dolls.

Meditation on early school years, six to ten years old:

Close your eyes and take several very deep, slow breaths. Let whatever you were doing before you sat down melt away like an ice cube melts in the sun. Plant your feet firmly on the floor and take everything off your lap. Take another deep breath, pulling air into your belly, making it extend in a Buddha belly breath. On the next breath, pull air way into your lungs, feel them expand with oxygen, and let this breath out slowly. Just let your breathing settle in as you relax. Now, picture yourself at the top of a staircase with ten steps down. As you take a step, hold the handrail that is there, take a deep breath, and picture yourself becoming younger and younger with each step down until at the last step you are age six to ten. Take a moment to allow your young self to speak to you. Ask this young you these questions:

1. In school interacting with others, what occurred that made an impression on you? Was there something that occurred as you did your schoolwork? Was there something that occurred

as you played and interacted with the other children? How did they treat you? Was there a teacher that made an impression on you, who told you something that you have carried with you? What message did you receive from your school experience or your family experience about who you were? How did that message and your experiences impact you and how you went about life at that age? Did you develop a part of yourself to cope or survive a situation or experience? How did you fit in with others? How did you fit in with your family? Ask about your relationship with your siblings. How were you treated by your brother and/or your sister, and what did they tell you about yourself? Ask your smaller self what was a decision or incident that influenced you at age six to ten years old? What occurred during those years that is still a part of you now?

2. Sit with your smaller self, and ask if there is anything that needs to heal, forgive, or release any negative feeling still lingering. Take a moment to be with her and hug her and let her know you are there for her now and forever. Surround this younger you with unconditional love and hugs. Just be with her for a few minutes and allow the healing tears, the love laughter, and your swelling heart and soul to envelop the moment. Tell her you can come back anytime she needs you, that you are going now but are never far away. Take a deep breath and return to the staircase. Take a breath and walk up the ten stairs. Take a deep breath at each stair until

you reach the top. Take one more deep breath and return to the room. Spend a few minutes journaling about what you learned from your younger self.

3. Once you have seen the younger self and the influence on your life today, go back to Bill Lamond's Completion Process for letting go of those things that no longer serve you as an adult.

Stirring the Pot

If events come up in your meditation that stir old wounds from your childhood and you have upset or anger toward someone in your life from that time, now is *not* the time to do any confronting. It is time to know that you were the one who saw the incident or event and made a decision about it. You are still carrying your feelings, emotions, and decisions into your adult life. They are locked away in your mental filing cabinet, ready to jump to attention when anything similar occurs and stirs those old feelings. It is up to you to take the steps to heal, forgive, or release the hold that the buried emotion has on you. If the incident was particularly painful and wounding, you may want to seek the professional assistance of a psychotherapist or hypnotherapist.

Change your parents, change your life.

Your parents do not have to change for you to design your own life. They do not have to understand or even be aware of how you were hurt or wounded.

It is all in how you have built it up in your own mind and consciousness. Your Mini-me made the choice to feel hurt and wounded. Yes, you were only nine at the time, but your nine-year-old self made a decision about life that has been running amok inside you. You are the only soul surgeon who can remove and heal that old black hole in your heart or soul. Proving someone wronged you or waiting for them to admit the wrong will not bring peace. Seeing how the wound has been buried and has grown tentacles into your present life is where the peace and empowerment comes. You are the one who will benefit from the healing and the completion, and your best revenge is to live your own life fully engaged and on your own joyous life path.

Meditation on early school years, eleven to eighteen years old:

Close your eyes and take several very deep, slow breaths. Let whatever you were doing before you sat down dissolve away. You can pick it up later. Plant your feet firmly on the floor and take everything off your lap. Take another deep breath, pulling air into your belly, making it extend in a Buddha belly breath. On the next breath, pull air way into your lungs, feel them expand with oxygen, and let this breath out slowly. Just let your breathing settle in as you relax. Now, picture yourself at the top of a staircase with ten steps down. As you take a step, hold the handrail that is there, take a deep breath, and picture yourself becoming younger and younger with each step down until at the last step you are age eleven to eighteen years old. These are the years when you are close to your adult self and your sexuality comes awake. Take a moment to allow your young self to speak to you. Ask this teenage you these questions:

1. What messages about your sexuality did you hear? What were you told or taught about your body? As you became a woman, developed breasts, and started your periods, how were you treated by your family? Your friends?

2. What role did you play as a teenager? Did you act out? Were you angry, misunderstood? A Goody Two-shoes? A smart student? A smartass? A popular kid? A nerd? A bad girl? Look at this role very carefully. Often feeling rejected as an emerging adult carves a very deep wound and keeps you stuck as an adult, still trying to make your teenage persona work. The famous inferiority complex can become instilled in your Mini-me, your ego, at this time in life. Ask the younger self what were their feelings during this period of life.

3. Who were your heroes? Who were your enemies? Who made you feel important and grown-up? Who made you feel inferior? Are you still using those old wounds to try to gain acceptance or avoid others today?

4. Ask your younger self what her high point was at this time in her life. What was the low point of this time in her life?

5. As you look at yourself as a high school graduate, what wisdom have you gained? What fears do you have about life? What messages from

your childhood are you carrying with you as a teenager?

6. What was your place in the cast of high school characters when you graduated? Class clown, class sweetheart, good girl, bad girl, smart girl, zoned-out girl? Jock? Cheerleader? Where did you fit or not fit? How has that part of life influenced who you are today? Are there any high school behaviors that are still a part of you as an adult? Have you been able to leave your teenage angst behind?

7. From that period in your life, when so many decisions about life are made, take an inventory of those life decisions that you made OR that someone made for you, such as these that I have heard ...

    ... you must go to law school because you are so smart; don't settle for being a teacher.

    ... all the boys in our family play football, are cheerleaders, are in _____ sorority/fraternity.

    ... you'll never make a real living as an artist, so go to college to get a well-paying job.

    .... college is not important; look at me—I never went to college.

    .... just go to trade school and get a job.

    .... I never went to college, so you *must* go to college.

Fill in your own

_____

8. Now, ask your younger self what is needed to heal and complete that time of life and to carry forward any useful wisdom but to let go of the bull you are hanging onto now as an adult. Use Bill Lamond's Completion Process on this stage of your life.

Meditation on early adult life, twenty-one to thirty years old:

Close your eyes and take several very deep, slow breaths. Let whatever you were doing before you sat down melt away in a puddle on the floor. Plant your feet firmly on the floor and take everything off your lap. Take another deep breath, pulling air into your belly, making it extend in a Buddha belly breath. On the next breath, pull air way into your lungs, feel them expand with oxygen, and let this breath out slowly. Just let your breathing settle in as you relax. Now, picture yourself at the top of a staircase with ten steps down. As you take a step, hold the handrail that is there, take a deep breath, and picture yourself becoming younger and younger with each step down until at the last step you are age twenty-one to thirty. Take a moment to allow yourself to speak to you. Ask this young you these questions:

1. Life has launched and you made some decisions about your adult life when you were younger. Are those decisions still serving you? Did you go to college and study what you wanted or what

was easy? Did you study what your parents wanted? What were you good at, at that time of life? Is that path working for you today? If you didn't attend college and went right to work, are you fulfilled where you are in your career? What dream or secret desire did you have about life then? Where is that dream or desire now? Have you married and started a family? Is that important to you? Is your relationship with your spouse or partner fulfilling for you both? If not, what is missing? What is your role with your parents? Are you still dependent on them to help you financially or emotionally? Are you really launched from your "mother ship" family of origin?

2. Where are you weak? Where do you let others and life roll over you? Where are you strong or tough in your life? Where have you let things roll along with no direction? What wisdom have you gained at this point in life? What sadness do you hold onto? What joy do you have about your life? At this time of life, are you where you thought you would be? What sidetracks have you taken?

3. What did you decide at this young adult age about life? Is that a valid decision today?

4. Look at this time of your life and write down the three most important things life has taught you thus far. Are those life lessons fear-based or expansion-based? This is a time of life when people get a bit beat up by life. Things are not working out as expected. Dreams are lost to pay

the rent. Discuss these ideas with your younger self, and list anything that needs to be dumped from your persona from this life stage. Go to Bill Lamond's Completion Process and take those things with you.

Meditation on adult life, thirty-one to forty years old:

Close your eyes and take several very deep, slow breaths. Let whatever you were doing before you sat down melt away. Plant your feet firmly on the floor and take everything off your lap. Take another deep breath, pulling air into your belly, making it extend in a Buddha belly breath. On the next breath, pull air way into your lungs, feel them expand with oxygen, and let this breath out slowly. Just let your breathing settle in as you relax. Now, picture yourself at the top of a staircase with ten steps down. As you take a step, hold the handrail that is there, take a deep breath, and picture yourself walking down these ten steps, taking a deep breath at each stair. See yourself at the bottom of the stairs at age thirty-one to forty. Take a moment to allow yourself to speak to you. Ask this you these questions:

1. How's it going in this time of life? Do you have a fulfilling career or vocation? Have you begun your family? Is a family something you desire in your life? At this time what has been the most important event in your life during this age? What is the reason this event is so important? What has been a low point during this age? What feeling about yourself and your

world came from that event? What did you decide about life, about yourself, and about your family? At this time in life, were you on a life path that you wanted and enjoyed? If not, why not? What did you tell yourself was the barrier? What skills or knowledge have you gained that you are using? What skills or knowledge were you missing? What gave you deep emotional satisfaction at this time of your life?

Life takes you like a lump of clay and molds you with experiences, challenges, significant emotional events, skinned knees, joys, and sorrows by this time of life. Write in your journal about some of these events in your life during this time and what you have gained as wisdom. What have you decided to fear? What have you decided is never going to happen that you longed for as a youth? During this period of your life, what needs to be extinguished that has been running you in the wrong direction? Go to Bill Lamond's Completion Process and remove any parts of this stage in your life that no longer serve you.

Middle life meditation, forty-one to sixty years old:

Close your eyes and take several very deep, slow breaths. Let whatever you were doing before you sat down melt away in a puddle on the floor. Plant your feet firmly on the floor and take everything off your lap. Take another deep breath, pulling air into your belly, making it extend in a Buddha belly breath. On the next breath, pull air way into your lungs, feel them expand with oxygen, and let this breath out slowly. Just let your breathing settle in as you relax. Now, picture yourself at the top of a staircase with ten steps down. As you take a step, hold the handrail that is there, take a deep breath, and picture yourself at the bottom of the stairs at age forty-one to sixty years old. Ask yourself these questions:

1. Did you reach middle age with power and passion in your life? Middle age is a big arena for the reassessment of life, love, career, place and finances. Many people take this time to try to recapture a missed youth—thus all the middle-aged Harley riders on the road. Many arrive at middle age, look around, and ask, "Is this all there is?" Some try to relive their glory days with obsessions with their favorite sports. Some look at a career well begun and see that the world has moved on and their skills are less valuable. This is a time to reassess and to redirect your life path if you are not feeling fulfilled in your career or your relationship.

2. Ask yourself these questions:

   What am I still longing for from my youth? Am I willing to give up the longing, or does that longing need a voice?

   What in my life is/was fulfilling?
   ... career?
   ... spouse and family?
   ... relationship with parents and extended family?
   ... finances?
   ... health?

... spirituality?

What in my life is/was not fulfilling?
   ... career?
   ... spouse and family?
   ... relationship with parents and extended family?
   ... finances?
   ... health?
   ... spirituality?

Write about each of these in your journal. Look at what you have to say about this time of life. What wisdom have you gained about this life now? Since you still have half a life to live what did you need to change that you did and what did you need to change that you still have not?

Regrets

This is the time of life to discuss the topic of regrets. Internet dictionary defines "regret" this way:

re·gret verb - feel sad, repentant, or disappointed over (something that has happened or been done, especially a loss or missed opportunity).

If you recall the Robert Frost poem "The Road Not Taken" from your school days, you will get the idea about regrets. Regrets can keep you frozen and keep you from your charmed life. Dreaming about a past path that could have been is a huge waste of time. Now, asking yourself what is the regret about is a better question. Consider any regrets in a new way.

What do you "think" you missed out on by not taking a step in your past? Often we build up a fantasy story about a choice we wished we had made. We paint a mental picture of an unreal ideal. Our mind, to keep us off our current path's potential, will cook up a delightful movie of the choice not taken becoming its own nirvana. If this is your regret, as Dr. Phil says it is time to "get real." Be responsible and grow this part of yourself up and into the present. You did not choose that. Here you are sucking the lifeblood out of your present, by living in a dream world of the past.

You have two choices: Go back and re-choose. Make it possible even if it feels challenging now. If you do this at least you will know you gave it all effort to make that missed opportunity work. Then, you can either enjoy going back to this regret with positive action. Or, you will see it was all a pipe dream and was not what you thought it would be.

> "In the long run, we shape our lives, and we shape ourselves. The process never ends until we die. And the choices we make are ultimately our own responsibility."
>
> Eleanor Roosevelt

What choice did you make that left the other choice still lingering in your mind? What did you do or say that you now feel was wrong or bad? Review any lingering regrets. Either take those regrets into a Completion Process. Clean out that closet in your mind. Or, reframe the missed opportunity into a new possibility. Remember: it is all about choices.

Chapter 3

Where do you want the path to go?

Chapter 3

Where do you want the path to go?

The Bible tells us that without a vision people perish. One of my early mentors, Paul J. Meyer, says:

"Whatever you vividly imagine, ardently desire, sincerely believe, and enthusiastically act upon must inevitably come to pass."

This important chapter for your charmed life design involves your mission and goal setting. The process here will help you clarify what you want so that it can "come to pass."

Imagine for now that you, as an individual, are a business named **You, Inc**. You are starting a new venture with You, Inc. The new venture is designed to create your own charmed life. This "You, Inc. Goal Setting Guide" is a process and format through which you become clear and specific about what you really want. You see, you are 100% responsible for your charmed life. You and your divine guidance source (God in my book of life) can create a charmed life.

The goal setting process that you will discover in this guide is a tool for today, AND it is a process that you can (and should) repeat. As you grow You, Inc, new opportunities will come along, old visions will fade, twists will show up along your path and take your breath away or twists can pull the rug out from under you. The You, Inc. path that you design now with the following pages provides you with a roadmap toward your charmed life. Use it now and bring it out at least once per year to repeat the purpose clarification and goal setting process.

In business and in life there is an overarching reason for being. There is a reason for being **you** in this world. For a business, there is a reason to be in business. That reason is encompassed in a vision, purpose or mission statement. A statement of WHY. This process of defining You, Inc starts with finding your own personal mission or purpose. Your purpose gives meaning to your goals which follow.

1. **Write your OWN personal mission, purpose statement.** Two authors, Dr. Steven Covey and Patrick Harbula, have helped me in this discovery

process. Since I want to honor each of them I am including them here for your research.

Dr. Steven Covey: Dr. Covey's book, *The 7 Habits of Highly Effective People,* has the best chapter ever on writing a personal mission statement. He says, "A mission statement is not something you write overnight. It takes deep introspection, careful analysis and thoughtful expression, and often many rewrites produce it in final form. ... it is a complete and concise expression of your innermost values and directions... your vision and values. It becomes the criterion by which you measure everything else in life."

Dr. Covey's book is a staple in my library. I have read and re-read his book many times. The chapter on writing a mission statement is "Habit # 2: Begin with the end in mind." Once you read Dr. Covey's chapter, carve out time for yourself to get in touch with YOU. This personal mission can involve your role in your family life, but it also is very personal about you. Until you are clear about what you want, it will be difficult to move yourself in a direction. Once you have a clear mission, you can then set the goals that will take you there.

Patrick Harbula: Patrick is my life coach, coach. He has a developed a different purpose identification process that he shares on his website www.livingpurposeinstitute.com. Go to the link, "Life Purpose Definition tool." You will find questions that will help you center in on your life's purpose. Patrick's book, *The Magic of the Soul*, is also a good guide to help you find your own soul's mission. His book includes several meditations on CD that can help you clarify your purpose.

If books are not your thing, then find a life coach (I am one. Contact me linda@lifepathbydesign.net). Whatever method you need to find a vision, mission, or purpose to follow, just do it. Your purpose, mission, or vision is the umbrella from which your goals follow. All your goals should align with your purpose.

Each year I take time to reread Dr. Covey's book or at least chapter 2. I review my mission statement and make any needed edits. One mission statement will not serve you for life. There may be a part of the mission that states your values that is constant. But your life changes over time. You will have a different mission statement when you are the mother of small children than you will have when you are an empty nester, or when you are close to retirement.

2. Set goals for your personal development and achievement.

As you proceed through the goal setting, you will need to ask yourself questions. Part of the reason people often do not get what they want in life is that they have not stopped to ask the right question. Coach yourself by taking your vision or mission and asking: what attributes, traits, skills, or education will you need to attain your vision?

The goals that you set are your own goals, not someone's idea of what you should be or do. Goals are the breakdown of the steps it takes to achieve your vision or to fulfill your purpose.

Here is an example: My stepdaughter decided in midlife that she needed a new vision and investigated several career options. Her vision was to be of service to others. She found a health-care degree she liked in occupational therapy. There is a competitive process to be accepted into the school she wanted to attend that offered her a master's degree. She also needed prerequisites since her other degree was in English; she needed several science courses. She set about not only taking the required courses, but looking at the program for occupational therapy assistants in the school she attended for her science courses. Occupational therapy assistant was her backup. She made friends with people in the OT department as she took her courses. Her efforts to find a program, obtain the prerequisites, and network herself allowed her to be accepted into the program she wanted.

> "Success is the progressive realization of worthwhile, predetermined personal goals."
>
> Paul J. Meyer, founder of Success Motivation Institute

The vision is your first step. If you are already in a career that you like, then find goals that will stretch you within that profession. As humans we function best with a bit of a challenge in our path. If the path becomes too routine or predictable, we can become complacent and bored.

Goals must include personal transformations through success habits. If you have not developed success habits, then this is a good time to start. What are success habits?

Read or listen to positive, uplifting books or magazines. One of my favorite magazines is *SUCCESS* magazine, which comes every month with a CD of great business and personal-growth ideas. Audible has books to download and listen to in your car or while you are getting dressed in the morning. (See Step 6 for more.)

3. Know why most people don't set goals and may not support your goals.

I was close to forty before I even knew the value of goal setting. Life was at a turning point for me, and I discovered goal setting. Life has become so much better over time and has continued to unfold my potential through continued goal setting.

Reasons people don't set goals:

Fear: Fear keeps people from setting goals. Fear comes into our mind in two areas:

1. Fear of Failure: *I am afraid I will set a goal and fail. Then, I will be a failure.*

2. Fear of embarrassment: *I am afraid of what others will think if I act like a big cheese and set goals.*

> "I think fearless is having fears and jumping anyway."
>
> Taylor Swift

Fear keeps people from setting goals. In truth, the actual goal is less important than the person you become as you go face the fears and go for your goals anyway. Have faith in an age-old success system of purpose clarification and goal setting, then plow forward to set your goals for your charmed life. (Read more about Fear in chapter 7.)

Skeptical: Some people are skeptical as to the value of goal setting. Skeptics often hide their own true potential from themselves and others by getting into the devil's advocate role. They won't try anything different from what they already do. Mostly, it is the same fear as we discussed earlier. When the skeptic pontificates about the idiocy of goal setting, they never face their own fear of failure or the fear of what others will think.

Don't know how: You are in luck because the following information in this guide will tell you how. Check that one off.

Don't want the pressure: Because I now live in California, I find that there is a gentle breeze of beach life, surfing, sun, and fun that seems to favor the attitude of "go with the flow." There are many people who do not want any pressure in their life. They do not want to take responsibility for "going for it." They may be OK with wherever they are in life. Guess what—if that is you, you are reading the wrong book. The rest of you, read on.

4. **Set balanced goals in all areas of your life:**
   Health/fitness
   Fun/vacation/recreation
   Personal development/education
   Friends/community
   Family/home
   Love/relationship
   Spiritual
   Career/business
   Wealth/finances
   Self-care

To help you see the areas in perspective, use the diagram of the "Wheel of Life" on the next page as a self-assessment. Mark on the "V" a line indicating where you are now. Are you at 50 percent on Family and 80 percent on Health & Fitness? To really give your wheel a visual understanding, take colored pencils and color in to the line that you have drawn. How does you wheel roll? An example of the Wheel filled in follows to give you an idea of how this visual can help you see your life in a new way.

Disclaimer: The "Wheel of Life" diagram original is a trademark of the Success Motivation Institute® used by permission. This "Wheel of Life" is my interpretation of areas that I have found make my life a charmed one. You may edit the categories for yourself. Add an area or remove one that does not resonate with you. Make this *your* Wheel of Life

Wheel of Life

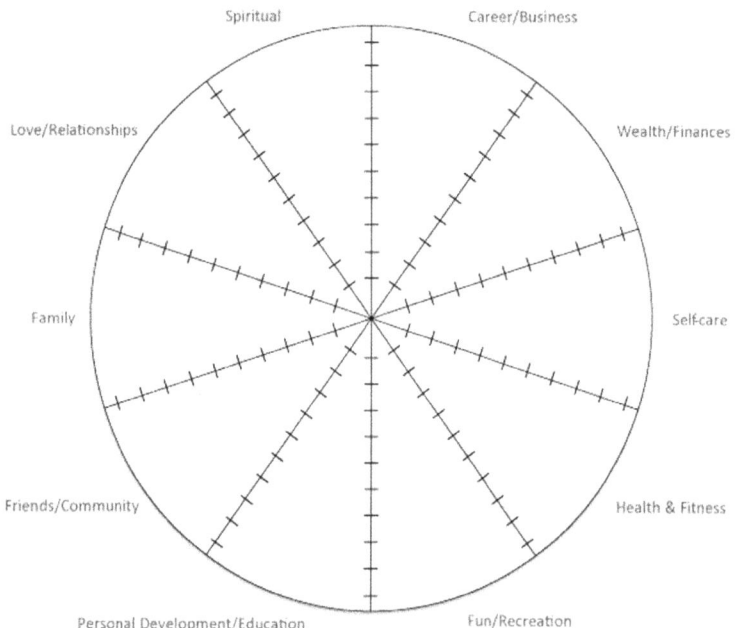

The "Wheel of Life" diagram original is a trademark of the Success Motivation Institute® used by permission.

Instructions: 1. Rename any of the sections.
2. Pick the line that represents where you are in that section and color in the piece of the pie.
3. Use the visual as you set your goals.

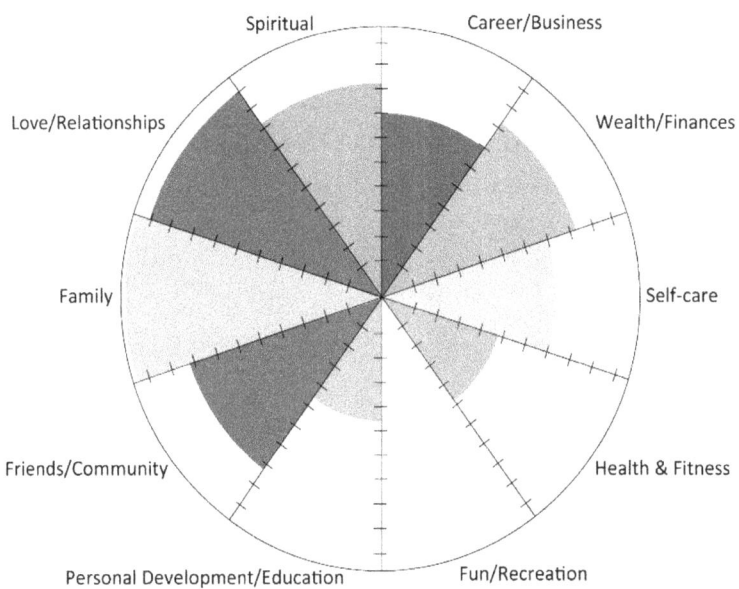

5. SMART Goal setting. Set goals that are:

Specific, **M**easurable, **A**chievable, **R**ealistic, and **T**imely.

Specific: Goals that swim around in your head are less likely to become a reality than those you write down.

Specific = Take the family on an outing twice per month.

Non-specific = Make the family happy.

Measurable: I weigh 140 pounds.

Not measurable: I will lose weight.

Achievable: You must be able to picture yourself attaining the goal.

Realistic: Though we can achieve what we believe, a goal has to be realistic.

Timely: Date your goals. Setting deadlines gives you a time requirement **Short-range goals: 6 months – 1 year**

Medium-range goals: 1 – 3 years

Long-range goals: 5 – 10 years

You, Inc. Goal-Setting Worksheet

Health & Fitness goals:

Short-range:

1. _____
2. _____
3. _____
4. _____

Medium-range:

1. _____
2. _____
3. _____
4. _____

Long-range:

1. _____
2. _____
3. _____
4. _____

Family/home goals:

Short-range:

1. _____
2. _____
3. _____
4. _____

Medium-range:

1. _____
2. _____
3. _____
4. _____

Long-range:

1. _____
2. _____
3. _____
4. _____

Friends/community Goals:

Short-range:

1. _____
2. _____
3. _____
4. _____

Medium-range:

1. _____
2. _____
3. _____
4. _____

Long-range:

1. _____
2. _____
3. _____
4. _____

> "Decide what you want, decide what you are willing to exchange for it. Establish your priorities and GO TO WORK!"
>
> H.L. Hunt

Wealth/financial Goals:

Short-range:

1. _____
2. _____
3. _____
4. _____

Medium-range:

1. _____
2. _____
3. _____
4. _____

Long-range:

1. _____
2. _____
3. _____
4. _____

Spiritual Goals:

Short-range:

1. _____
2. _____
3. _____
4. _____

Medium-range:

1. _____
2. _____
3. _____
4. _____

Long-range:

1. _____
2. _____
3. _____
4. _____

> "Setting goals is the first step in turning the invisible into the visible."
>
> Tony Robbins

Career/business Goals:

Short-range:

1. _____
2. _____
3. _____
4. _____

Medium-range:

1. _____
2. _____
3. _____
4. _____

Long-range:

1. _____
2. _____
3. _____
4. _____

Fun/vacation/recreation goals:

Short-range:

1. _____
2. _____
3. _____
4. _____

Medium-range:

1. _____
2. _____
3. _____
4. _____

Long-range:

1. _____
2. _____
3. _____
4. _____

Personal development/education goals:

Short-range:

1. _____

2. _____

3. _____

4. _____

Medium-range:

1. _____

2. _____

3. _____

4. _____

Long-range:

1. _____

2. _____

3. _____

4. _____

Love/relationship goals:

Short-range

1. _____
2. _____
3. _____
4. _____

Medium-range:

1. _____
2. _____
3. _____
4. _____

Long-range:

1. _____
2. _____
3. _____
4. _____

> "Learn from the past, set vivid, detailed goals for the future, and live in the only moment of time over which you have any control: now."
>
> Denis Waitley

Self-care goals:

Short-range:

1. _____
2. _____
3. _____
4. _____

Medium-range:

1. _____
2. _____
3. _____
4. _____

Long-range:

1. _____
2. _____
3. _____
4. _____

6. Overcome your own excuses, fears, and barriers, and find a way to move to action.

> "A journey of a thousand miles begins with a single step"
>
> Laozi, Chinese philosopher

Feed yourself *good* mind food. Read inspirational books, magazines and online blogs.

Listen to an inspirational MP3 or audiobook or upbeat music every morning. Watch what you read and listen to. Avoid TV violence, bad news headlines, and soap operas.

Avoid the evening news before bed; read something positive.

Find positive people to associate with, people who will stretch you.

Eliminate/avoid/lessen the time you spend with negative or toxic people.

Build your self-discipline quotient.

Act boldly.

7. Review progress and reset goals regularly.

Remember goal GETTING takes commitment. The following is from Zig Ziglar's *See You at The Top:*

"I, _____, am serious about setting and reaching my goals in life. I promise myself that I will take the first steps toward setting and reaching those goals.

I am willing to forego temporary pleasures in the pursuit of happiness and to strive for excellence in my goal-setting efforts. I am willing to discipline my physical and emotional appetites to reach the long-range goals that I have set.

I recognize that to reach my goals I must grow personally and have the right mental attitude, so I promise to specifically increase my knowledge in my chosen field and regularly read positive growth books and magazines. I will also attend lectures and seminars, take courses in personal growth and development, and utilize my time more effectively by listening to motivational and educational recordings.

Persistence and commitment are prerequisites to reaching any goal, so I promise myself that I am going to faithfully work on my goals EVERY day. I will chart my progress and recommit myself to my direction!"

Download the e-booklet You, Inc. Goal-Setting Guide on my website www.lifepathbydesign.net

> "Man, with God's help and personal dedication, is capable of anything he can dream."
>
> Conrad Hilton

Chapter 4

What stones are in your path?

Chapter 4

What stones are in your path?

Stones in your path are distractors. They can show up to throw you off your life path, stop you dead in your tracks, or cause you to seriously doubt the path you have started. In fact, if you start to move yourself in the direction of your goals and your vision, you know you are on the right track when the stones show up. Knowing that stones are apt to be there and having your own defense tools will make the path easier. You can use the tools in this chapter plus your guts and your faith to defend against two big life path stones: A.N.T.s and THEY.

Your tools will help you guard against your own negativity and any negativity from well-meaning others. Spoiling your resolve, creating doubt, and squashing your motivation is the game played by A.N.T.s, **A**utomatic **N**egative **T**houghts, and THEY. One at a time or in tandem, these buggers are stones that you will want to send packing.

A.N.T.s

A.N.T.s, show up for all of us. You would not allow ants to infest your home, would you? Besides being pests, ants sneak into nooks and crannies. Just when you get them out of the kitchen, they show up in the bathroom.

A.N.T.s can infest your mind. These Automatic Negative Thoughts can rob your potential AND your motivation. Your mind left uncontrolled will take you on a ride you will not be happy with in the end.

Do you work out, go to the gym, walk, or run to take care of yourself? Do you floss and brush your teeth? (This one is important to me since I am a dental hygienist.) Do you watch what you eat (most of the time) to be sure to get your nutrients? We are often so good with these good health disciplines, yet we let our mind run wild. Our mind can even create wildfires of crisis to keep us fed with an emotional charge.

You are in control of your mind. Repeat this to yourself several times:

I am in control of my mind.

Yep, no doubt about it. It's your baby; you birthed it. You have grown it to its current place in your cranium. You have fed it all its life. But hey, who is in the control tower? Do you have a past? Have you been hurt? Have you had some bumps in the road? Are you in a ditch right now?

Life doesn't trip us up; it is the A.N.T.s that we let run loose about the event or about those people who did something to us or who are doing it to us still. We have an initial Automatic Negative Thought, we believe that to be the truth, and we act/react on that thought. That A.N.T. grows.

Let me ask you a couple of questions: Have you ever thought any of the following: my husband doesn't show me enough attention; my boss cares only about the money I bring in; my mother-in-law has never liked me. You see where I am going? Write down one A.N.T. that you know is in your mind. Then ask yourself, as author of "The Work," Byron Katie does, "Is it really true?" Sometimes we cook things up in our undisciplined mind, and we act as if it were true. Look at your A.N.T.s and ask this question: do I feel powerful when I think that, or do I feel powerless? If the answer is a negative feeling, you have my permission to squash that A.N.T.

When A.N.T.s run loose in your mind, the job of controlling them or silencing their chatter can seem a bit overwhelming. Here are some A.N.T. squashing tools:

Talk to your A.N.T.

Learn to talk to your A.N.T.s *Oh, my gosh, where is she going with this?* you might ask. The first step in recovering your full potential is awareness. When you are aware of the A.N.T., the battle to rid yourself of them is half-won.

You notice an A.N.T., so you stop and ask, "Miss A.N.T., what is this all about? Is there something I need to handle or that I have not looked at? Or are you just being a pest?" Doing this allows you to honor the fact that the A.N.T. is trying to protect you from something, though many times the A.N.T. is your ego trying to keep you in you "Same" place, worried, fearful and powerless. Then follow up with, "Thank you for sharing, but I have got this handled." Facing the A.N.T.s can dissolve their swarming abilities.

Affirmations

Affirmations are powerful tools against A.N.T.s. According to the *Internet Dictionary,* the word "affirm" means "to state or assert positively; maintain as true: to confirm or ratify: to assert solemnly: to express agreement with or commitment to; uphold; support." Affirmations are used to assert an idea positively. Affirmations express an alignment with your commitment to your path. Affirmations are tools to support you. They help you reprogram negative thinking and keep your mind focused on your desired outcome.

Think of affirmations as a tool to help retrain your mental autopilot and to flood your mind with positive thoughts, displacing the A.N.T. Your mental autopilot can steer you toward a ditch. Use the power of affirmations to help you stay the course and to reprogram your autopilot. Your autopilot has gathered strength over your entire life. The best illustration of this is a beautiful song from the '50s movie *South Pacific*. John Kerr, who plays Lt. Cable, sings the song. He has fallen in love with an Asian woman, a big "no-no" in his New Jersey family in the time of WWII. He sings the song to nurse Nellie, who has fallen in love with a Frenchman. Read these words and see if they give you any insights about your autopilot.

You've got to be taught

To hate and fear,

You've got to be taught

From year to year,

It's got to be drummed

In your dear little ear.

©Songwriters: Rogers and Hammerstein

    The song refers to learning to hate people of a different culture. Our family of origin, the people who influence us from birth through our young years, usually until we are about eight to ten, teach us how to look at the world. After about age ten, peers take over the role of "telling" us who to like and dislike and who we are. That programing is our autopilot. Therefore, when you are ready to step out of that programed role, your A.N.T.s come in big black swarms. Use affirmations as your tool to combat any Automatic Negative Thoughts.

The Affirmation Tool Kit

How to write and use affirmations.

First – Affirmations are short—only one tight sentence.

Second – Affirmations are positive statements. Leave out negatives.

Third – Affirmations use an active, present verb.

Fourth – Affirmations describe who you want to be and/or what you want to do in your life.

Fifth – Affirmations are specific.

Sixth – Write your affirmation using "I" or "My." The "I am" verbiage is an age-old way to create a statement that resonates with your subconscious.

> Use Affirmations to Replace A.N.T.s

Ways to use your affirmations: Flood your mind with the affirmation. Write the affirmation on a "3 X 5" card or a sticky note. Say the affirmation aloud or silently to yourself 100 times per day. Read and repeat the affirmations, especially first thing as you arise and last thing before you go to sleep. Keep the affirmation on a sticky note or card at your computer, in your pocket, on the mirror where you get ready in the morning and on your car's dashboard. Make the affirmation into a screen saver.

Here are several fill-in-the-blank affirmations and some samples.

Creating Affirmations:

Formula for writing an affirmation:

I am committed to (an action) in order to (outcome you want) by (target date) because (why?).

I am committed to writing four hours per week to have my book completed by January 15, 2016, so that I am a published author.

Example: I am a successful author.

I am _____

Example: You, Linda Drevenstedt, are cultivating potential in people.

You, __ (your name) _____ are_____

My life path includes_____

My income on (date) is $_____

Other samples:

I am on my best life path.

I am free to be my best self.

I am open to all my possibilities.

I show appreciation to the people in my life.

I express positive qualities.

I am open to prosperity, doing what I love, and making money.

I attract loving people in my life.

I see God's perfection in everyone.

Remember, the affirmations you write for your specific, pesky A.N.T.s gives you the most oomph. Just remember to state the affirmation in positive terms.

THEY

Data on *Star Trek* was an android, a computer-generated being. Periodically, one of Data's computer chips would malfunction, and his behavior would change. The chip had to be repaired or replaced so that Data could function at his high level.

We, too, have soft tissue chips that often malfunction and need a repair or replacement. One of the damaged chips many of us carry around is the "they" chip. This chip in its malfunction can ruin and run our lives and keep us from our own charmed life path. "THEY" are the good opinions of others in our lives that we carry in our head and in our heart, that we listen to over coffee. Often, we proceed through life unaware of the influence "THEY" have on our behavior, our feelings, and our thoughts.

The "THEY" voice is programmed into our soft tissue chip early in life. The scripts, expectations, and programming that "THEY" give us become visceral integrations into our being, often without our conscious knowledge. We spend a lifetime gathering our self-esteem and self-image from "THEY." Then, as we step into our own life path, those impressions and comments come back into view OR the people in our life repeat the comments so that we feel we are, in fact, what THEY are saying. We cannot seem to avoid the message.

THEY say: you ...

> ... are clumsy, awkward.
>
> ... will never amount to much.
>
> ... are beautiful.
>
> ... are always sick.
>
> ... eat too much.
>
> ... must clean your plate.
>
> ... can't spell, can't _____.
>
> ... are not good at math.
>
> ... shouldn't be a musician; it is a dead end; you'll never make a living.
>
> ... are a slow reader.
>
> ... are so much smarter than anyone else.
>
> ... have no rhythm.
>
> ... can't trust "those" people.
>
> ... can't do that; your children are so young.
>
> ... had better be good because God, the bogeyman, etc. is watching.
>
> ... are too old, too young, too flighty, too irresponsible, too short, too _____.
>
> ..._____

Terry Cole-Whittaker's book, *What You Think of Me IS None of My Business*, changed my life on this topic. If THEY are running your life, especially well-meaning family and friends, I highly recommend that you stop right now, go to Amazon, and order Terry's book. Devour it and come back here.

If you have been on the path and you just need a booster shot to get back to your path, then use this quote from Eleanor Roosevelt that I use as an affirmation:

> "No one can make you feel inferior without your consent."

Ultimately, the defense against A.N.T.s and THEY is your faith in yourself, your connection to a higher power for strength, and your ability to develop guts to strike out on your own path.

Create your own supporting symbols or icons as reminders to you about the strength other women have used to walk their paths. On the wall of my office for years, I kept a Norman Rockwell picture of Rosie the Riveter. She was my visual heroine who blazed a new path. The cartoon of Wonder Woman is another icon I keep handy. I look for books about "strong women making it through difficulties." My favorite books are in the "Resources" section at the end of the book. They are all good mind food to keep your spirits and resolve up as you face A.N.T.s and THEY.

Chapter 5

Why are there twists and turns in my path?

Chapter 5

Why are there twists and turns in my path?

I beg your pardon

I never promised you a rose garden

Along with the sunshine

There's gotta be a little rain sometime.

Written by Joe South and made famous in recordings by Lynn Anderson in the 1970s and by Martina McBride in 2005.

    Country songs tell you that life and love have a fickle sense of humor and drama, yet life is neutral;

it provides us with sunshine and rain. How we come to terms with life's left turns is part of Life Path by Design. Maybe life has given you a hurricane, dashed dreams, a lost job in middle age, a business closure, an unfulfilling degree path, the loss of a lover or spouse, children who disappoint you, or many of the other life happenings. How can you navigate through and come out with a remapped sense of yourself?

Instead of "Why me?" I was introduced to a better question. My dream business was a successful consulting firm with a training center where dentists and their teams could come for classes. From 1992, when I started my business, until 2001, when I closed the doors to my training center, I worked with every sinew in my body and soul to make my business successful. I did what I thought were the RIGHT things to make it successful. My advisors helped me navigate accounting and legal matters, and I had my own personal development coach. I dutifully prayed, attended church, and tithed. So why had God, life, fate brought me to my knees in a long dark night of the soul? Why? Why? Why? I railed at the universe. I was to learn that was not the question to ask. There was a better question.

When 9/11 happened, the entire country went into panic and then cocooned. No one wanted to travel to attend classes at my training center. I worked myself into exhaustion to try to keep the doors open—I can do WORKAHOLIC with the best of them—but all my efforts did not work. I could not afford the rent and the salaries to support the center. When I closed the doors, I went into a deep adult pity party. I could not understand how, if I had done the "right" things, this could happen. I blamed myself. Surely there was something else "I" could have done. I blamed God for letting me down when I had been a lifelong God supporter. How could this be happening?

Ask better questions

Here is the question that helped me navigate the left turn that life gave me. I had lunch with my good friend Dr. David Reznik. I proceeded to blubber on about my woes and disappointments, on and on. We happened to be at a restaurant that had butcher paper as the tablecloth. We were given crayons to draw, and the waiter had come along, introduced himself, and wrote his name on the paper. Next, a life-changing moment came from something that only a true friend would do. Dave took the crayon and drew a big question mark.

Then he asked, "Linda, what are you going to get out of life that you could not have if the training center had stayed open?"

I burst into tears and blubbered that I would have more time with Ted (my husband who is nine years my senior). In that split second, with Dave's question, my life for the past few years flashed before me. The stress of building my dream business had taken a toll on my health and stolen time with my family. My left turn was now in front of me had a different point of view. It all came in the flash of a question.

Dr. Dave is a student of the question. He has studied both in the corporate world and in the spiritual world. He helped me understand ... the Art of the Question.

What can you do to pick up the pieces of a dashed life dream? Have you dreamed that you would ride off into the sunset with Prince Charming and then find yourself divorced? Did you think the career path you spent twelve years educating yourself for would be fulfilling and then find out, NOT?

Left turns can either empower you to move onto a new path, or they can toss you over, causing you to spend your life pining away for the loss rather than recover, reboot, and re-engage in a new life path, a new choice. The challenge you'll face is to leave the bitterness, blame, and self-torture behind.

Blame

Blame is a trick our ego plays on us so that we either do not have to either deal with reality or own up to our part in the situation. Your ego wants to protect you from taking responsibility for the situation that is causing you pain, grief, sleepless nights, anguish, anger, boredom, frustration, and many other negative emotions and feelings. Soul sickness can come wrapped in an enticing package of blame. Also, we live in an American culture that is addicted to drama, so there are plenty of supporters for your blame story.

Righteous blaming is an elusive shield our ego uses. Life Path by Design requires a different process and other tools. Taking 100 percent responsibility for your life is the path toward soul growth and peace. "But ... but ... but ...," you might say, "but what about the wrong, the injustice, the letdown?"

It takes being 100 percent responsible first, which often requires a bit of humble pie. Choice is the answer.

> You always have a choice.

Take your current unhappiness, sense of loss, or lack of drive, fulfillment, or passion, and ask yourself these questions:

- What choices are open to me now that I did not see before this left turn came into my path?
- Did I ignore some warning signs?
- Did I choose not to speak up for myself ... not to set boundaries?
- What in this situation is familiar or has happened before?

List at least three things that you are now able to do or could do because of this left turn.

Spend a meditation time asking your inner self when this type of situation has happened before in your life. What were the feelings you had then? Did blaming resolve those feelings then? Do you feel neutral about the situation, or does the thought of that situation mentally take you for an emotional ride?

If you look back and see a pattern of similar situations, then you need to clean this up in order to have the life you want. Meditate and then journal about the current situation. Settle in on your feelings. Now, ask yourself when the last time was that you felt those same feelings.

A blame story can haunt you and steal your joy. You can carry blame like a Linus blanket following you around. When life gets tough—the rains come, the lover leaves, the job goes away—you bring out the blame story to protect your own ego from taking full responsibility and to avoid the overwhelming sad emotions. Some wounds or life events take a while to heal; however, healing is retarded by blame. You stay in victim consciousness when you blame. A wound or a hurt can be buried under layers like onion layers. They may keep showing their ugly head until you get a deep, full healing.

Two people have helped me with this process: Dr. Michael Ryce and Bill Lamond. Both will tell you that there is no magic pill, but if you are willing to do the work with their tools, you can peel the blame or hurt onion, one layer at a time.

Dr. Michael Ryce first helped me shift from blame to claiming my voice and finding my personal power after my divorce. Most people who go through a divorce blame someone else for their pain and troubles. It is human nature. Even if you left someone, you blame them for not being the person you thought you married. I fell right into the ego trap of blaming my former spouse for not being the person "I" wanted and expected him to be. I went headlong into the role of dutiful wife and mother. Twenty years later with ten moves under my belt, I was done, and I left with a pocketful of righteous blame. He did not fulfill my dream, so it had to be his fault, right?

Dr. Ryce gave me the ticket to a left turn and to get out of "blame jail." Getting REAL with this part of my life opened my life to living with what Tony Robbins calls "passion." If you know you are allowing blame to keep you from your own peace, serenity, passion, and love, then take the next step. Blame stories are quite cancerous in many families. You may want a guide or a coach to help you move out of using blame to protect yourself from the real deal, which is that you have/had a choice.

If you want a "Do It Yourself" recovery from blame, go directly to Dr. Michael Ryce's website: www.whyagain.org. Order Dr. Ryce's CD set *Why Is This Happening to Me Again?"* or find a workshop that he is giving in your area.

Tackling blame is your own "Get out of Jail Free" card. It is worth your time and dedicated investment to clean up blame in your life. And, just like dirty dishes, blame will show up again and creep back into your thinking quicker than a flash. Staying in ownership of your life takes guts. The reason this book is called *Life Path by Design* is that most people allow life to move them along as if they were in rapids on the river without a boat or a paddle. You are your own paddle, oar, rudder, and life vest. You and your alignment with your inner guide, your God, your higher power are the superpower to move you along the healing path.

Ask yourself the next time blame comes into your viewfinder: "What have I said (or not said) in this situation that, if I made a new choice to take care of myself, might make things different?"

Did I forget to ...?

... speak my own true voice?

... get control over my emotions before I bark out to others the rage I feel so that they can't even hear me?

... set a boundary to take care of myself?

... keep a boundary that I have set?

Learning to move or stay out of blame when life hands you a left turn and gives you lemons is a skill you need in order to create a charmed life. You need to always be ready to follow this saying:

> When life hands you lemons, make lemonade.

Chapter 6

What is this pain telling you?

Chapter 6

What is this pain telling you?

You learned in the prior chapters that there are many things that can throw you off your life path. Pain can take you down, but pain is trying to tell you something. Your quest, when you are in pain, is to discover the message. The long, dark night of the soul—psychic pain, mental anguish, lost soul despair, physical pain, even the "deep dark depression and excessive misery" as the Buck Owens song lyric goes—it all comes to visit each of us at some time along our life path. I love what Fran Drescher, *The Nanny*, says in her book *Cancer Schmancer*: "**No one** leaves this planet **unscathed.**"

When you are up against pain at any time in your life, it is a signal for you to ask questions. Is it time to reassess your life path? Pain can be the equivalent of a life path fork in the road. Old pains can, in fact, become an albatross companion. Old pains can be physical, such as an old injury from an accident. Old pains can be from your heart and soul, such as a broken heart when your lover left or you had a large life disappointment such as the death of someone close to you. All of those old pains become buried in your cells. Pain comes from a story you continue to tell yourself about an original hurt or disappointment. The story takes on a life of its own. It can become the filter through which you view the present.

Have you gone so deep into your story of the original incident that it has become a part of your body story? These old wounds are deep gashes into your soul's light and life.

What is the pain message?

When you are in pain, it is your job to ask enough deep, soul-level questions to uncover the message. Old pains and wounds are like a backpack that you carry. In the present, old wounds are just under the surface, waiting for the next opportunity to prove again how deeply you were originally wounded. This backpack full of old hurts sits in front of you and becomes your barrier to a full life. You greet everyone and every event from behind the backpack.

The mental game of pain is initially one to get your attention. "Hmm, something doesn't feel right here," your mind might say. If you are either physically or emotionally small at the time, you fall victim to the pain. This can set up a repeated pattern because you have not been able at that time to hear the message of the pain or to be emotionally strong enough to move through the pain to find the origin and the message.

Perfect parents are a myth

Adults often carry wounds from childhood. We carry an ideal parent in our head and compare that to our real parents or caregivers.

We tell ourselves that if only he/she had been different then my life would be great. We hide out in a mental conversation with our self and avoid the work we may need to do to heal old wounds. Inner-child healing is its own body of research and work, and that is not the purpose of this book. However, if in the process of reading and meditating, you discover any deep, old childhood wounds, then get thee to a healer. One I recommend considering is Brandon Bays author of *The Journey*. (see Resources)

Over my life path I have benefitted greatly from hypnotherapy, Gestalt, Kabala, guided imagery coaching, NLP (neurolinguistic programming of Tony Robbins fame), and my own meditation. When you do not heal the old wound, you go unaware into your world wearing the backpack in front of you as a barrier for protection. That barrier keeps you from being present, whole, and free on your life path. If you keep adding to the backpack with new wounds that you choose not to heal, then your own life burden becomes very heavy; this is where depression can become the life path you trudge.

Physical pain is a message. Louise Hay quantified pain messages and their meaning in her book *Heal Your Body*. Western medicine is less inclined to ask you to get still and listen to your body, yet years ago when I was having knee pain, my coach asked me to meditate on my knee. He asked me to picture the knee sitting in a chair and to ask it: "What is the problem, knee?" Weird, I know, but I got the message. At the time, I was afraid to quit my job and start my own business. My knee was immobilizing me and taking me off track. It was my excuse for why I couldn't start a business. My knee was a cosmic messenger. It was my subconscious fear of moving forward in a new direction.

When I addressed the fear about quitting my job AND getting back to the gym despite the discomfort, I was able to move forward. It took time to craft a plan to secure enough consistent income on a part-time basis so that I could start my consulting business. The plan that came about turned out to be perfect for my life path at the time. I knew a top-notch dentist near my home; I had been a temporary dental assistant in his office when I moved to Atlanta after my divorce. I called and asked to take him to lunch, and then I shared my goal of starting my own consulting firm. To start the business I needed an income to keep up my car payment and pay my son's college expenses. The amount was the equivalent of working two days as a dental hygienist. I asked if he had an opening in his practice.

When you are on your path, divine providence steps in to move you along. He said he would make room for me. Dr. Bill Williams gave me the privilege of working in, by far, the most advanced practice I knew. My time there was an eye-opening education.

What pain is keeping you from your life path? What is slowing you down or getting in your way? Is it mind games you are playing with yourself? Is it fears you have not been willing to face? Is it worry and procrastination? Is there an old wound that needs to be healed?

Take out your journal and write a letter, asking your pain what the message is. Keep journaling until you find your answer. It is there, and only you can unlock the message the pain is bringing to you. Use this tool anytime you are in pain.

Chapter 7

Can you handle life's dementors?

Chapter 7

Can you handle life's dementors?

Pain, left turns, stones, and now dementors. Yes, your Life Path by Design can bump into a variety of pests that can take you off track. Your ability to coach yourself out of, away from, over, or under these distractors is a key to living your own charmed life. There are plenty of littered lives out there. People got caught in the distractor and stopped their own life path; they settled; they wimped out; they went back to the old way—just because they were unwilling to tackle what lay before them. You will be ready to handle your distractors. This chapter gives you more for your coaching tool kit.

Dementors

You can guard your potential and your life path against what, in Harry Potter's world, are the Dementors. According to the *Harry Potter Wiki*: "Dementors are ghostly creatures who are foul. ... They feed upon human happiness, and thus cause depression and despair to anyone near them." Dementors are those mental ghosts that show up as you begin to go for it.

There are major dementors and minor dementors. Major dementors are

Fear, Anger, and Worry

On your life path, as you are learning to move, motivating yourself through change is an essential skill. Using more of your potential requires a change in your internal GPS, your global positioning system. As you change, you need to adjust how you see yourself in your world. Your ability to become an expert change agent is an essential part of your Life Path by Design Tool Kit.

Why is change so difficult for most people? It is based on B.S.*

B.S.* Controls your life

B.S.* Belief System

Your mind, your conscious and subconscious brain, creates your life, your reality, your perception. Your brain is full of information that has been stored for your whole lifetime. From birth you have been gathering data in your mind, your brain. Much of the data has been stored without censor, without review, without judgment, and without your conscious knowledge.

As you experience life, only a small percent of your life is controlled by your conscious mind. Most of life is controlled by your subconscious mind. Some experts say as much as 90 percent of all our actions, feelings, and thoughts come from our subconscious mind. The subconscious mind is the repository of all your impressions, opinions, fears, feelings, and experiences—what you saw and what you heard. It is all there. As I discussed in chapter 3, impressions that you received as a child, as a boy or as a girl, as a grammar school or high school student, as a churchgoer, as a scout, as a sibling; impressions you received from what you have read or studied—all of it is still there.

Often the deepest impressions are things that created deep emotional feelings at the time of the occurrence. For example, if you were scolded or spanked for getting your clothes dirty as a child, you may hold that feeling, that impression, in your subconscious mind. In your present life, that subconscious impression can reoccur as you go about your life as an extreme neat freak or just being a clean, neat person.

All impressions are stored, and your present actions emerge from that subconscious imprinting and filter. This process has no judgment about the value of the impression; the impression is merely stored—just as a copy machine does not evaluate the value of what you copy. You can copy great poetry or you can copy pornography. Your mind does not evaluate the data, particularly when you are young. As you grow into your teenage years and adulthood, those impressions form who you are and how you act. Your opinions are based on those early impressions. You are taught by those who impress you: parents, bosses, professors, Scout leaders, role models (both positive and negative), religious leaders, relatives, siblings, peers, acquaintances—anyone with whom you interact. Even external events can give you stored impressions: TV, magazines, public figures, media heroes and heroines.

As you grow your potential, begin to fulfill your purpose or mission, and go for your goals on your life path, you bump into your own dementors or subconscious patterns. You will find the "voices in your head and under your bed," as Eminem sings in his rap song "Monsters." These dementors emerge as you begin to change or challenge those impressions that are no longer serving you. The ones that show up to challenge you are often keeping you from your potential, holding you hostage to your past.

B.S. (Belief System) Reframing Tool Kit

This powerful exercise helps to reveal your major life influencers, both the positive and the negative. To continue on your life path, complete the following exercise.

Take out a sheet of paper and answer the following questions:

1. Make a list of the people who most influenced you as you grew up.

2. List the attributes and/or qualities these people taught or showed you. List both positive and negative qualities.

3. Which of each of these qualities in your opinion is positive?

   Put a "+" by it.

4. Which of each of these attributes in your opinion is negative?

   Put a "—"by it.

To date, your B.S. has been randomly programmed—nonselective, like a computer GIGO (Garbage In, Garbage Out), some good, some bad, some useful, some useless. Your current programming has been on autopilot without a pilot. All the impressions and feelings are stored in your B.S., Belief System. An example comes from years of working with high-achievement dentists who have been taught to be perfectionists. If you, too, are a perfectionist, read on. This high-achievement perfectionist can often grow from these impressions:

Childhood – strict discipline with strong verbal or physical punishment for making mistakes; parent gave conditional love with lots of "shoulds" and "oughts."

School – pressure to perform at school with little praise unless you made an "A"

College – push to have high grades to get into graduate school, little praise from professors

Career – have a high-paying, prestigious career; make Mama proud.

This example often translates into the following present-day B.S.

1. Strict on self to perform, perfectly.

2. Judgment of others who don't perform perfectly.

3. Anger at self for not being perfect, anger at others for not meeting high expectations.

4. Procrastination: fear of not doing something right, fear of disapproval or not doing "it" perfectly, and so avoid doing it.

5. Fear of disapproval from others.

6. Low self-esteem due to not measuring up ALL the time.

7. Worry over the past, the present, and the future actions and outcomes.

8. Worry over not making other people happy; if someone in your life is not happy, you hold the feeling that it is your fault and that it is your job to make "them" happy.

Does any of that sound familiar? It seems to be a human condition for many. How do you break free of your B.S.? You decide to change your mind. The precursor for change is a dissatisfaction with the way things are. If you have a sense of dissatisfaction with the things on your list, read on.

Your B.S. and the pride that your B.S. builds up in your mind to protect your ego from that dreadful thought "I've been wrong about _____" are what have kept you from making the change before now. What is wrong is the false B.S. that someone or something **other than YOU** has to do the changing in order for you to be OK.

People are often desperate to change their circumstances and think that other people or circumstances must change for them to get their life's desire.

> The only person you can change is YOU.

You are not going to change other people. All you can change is the gray matter between your ears. Taking 100 percent responsibility for your current situation, where you are now, is the first step. No one did it to you or made you do or be anything. You will keep yourself from your heart's desire if you stay in excuses or keep thinking that others have to do the changing.

The following dementors or barriers can keep you stuck in your current situation. Work with the exercises to learn to move yourself over, under, around, or through these barriers. Once you can lead yourself through one of these dementors, you will gain power to tackle another and then another. Pretty soon, you will have your own life path back.

1. **Anger**
2. **Fear**
3. **Worry**

The journey you take to learn to conquer, control, reduce, reframe, and/or eliminate these three dementors will build your life path muscle. You build life path muscle as you grow your ability to carry out a resolution, action, or activity long after the mood or initial spurt or desire has left. Ben Franklin gives us the best advice, "Resolve to perform that which you ought. Perform without fail that which you resolve." ***Keep on keeping on*** is the modern twist on Ben Franklin's quote.

ANGER

Anger gurgling from your judgment of yourself and others will keep you from peace and love and from living a charmed life. Here is how to quell anger:

Write a family profile of how anger was handled as you grew up. How did your father, your mother, and your siblings handle anger? How did you as a child handle your anger? Did you stuff it, act like nothing happened, throw temper tantrums, sulk, scream, yell, destroy things, cry, withdraw, carry a chip on your shoulder, shun those who angered you, talk about others (not to them), judge others who made your angry, decide you were better than others, and/or decide you didn't like/need those who made you angry?

How do you handle anger now as an adult? Is there a connection to your family or origin? Is the way you currently handle anger working for you now?

Unhealed anger spots become like festering subconscious pus pockets. Then, a particular person or situation makes you angry and the pus pocket bursts. You verbally spew your poison OR you stuff the anger and develop anxiety, high blood pressure, stomach problems, and even depression. Depression is often silent, unhandled anger.

You may need to repeat the following process, and you may decide to seek professional guidance through some anger work, especially if you know you harbor unresolved anger from your past. Believe it or not, that harbored, unresolved anger will keep you from leading a charmed life. Writing all of this out is part of the reprogramming process. This anger worksheet is part of your life path tool kit.

Anger Worksheet

Name: _____

Write out what they did to make you angry. Then answer the following questions: How does my anger at this person affect my life? What have been the negative consequences to:

... my personal relations with this person?

... my personal relationships with others I care about?

... my sense of well-being, peace, and self-worth?

... my physical health?

... my relationship with a higher power?

... my growth as a self-actualizing person?

Has this situation (reason for anger but perhaps another person) happened before? If this has happened before, am I willing to change to break the pattern, even if other people never change, admit what they did to me, or are even aware I was angry? How does holding on to this old anger benefit me now, today?

There is always a payoff to staying angry. When you hold anger toward another, you stay connected to that person via unresolved anger. Ask yourself this: am I willing to do the inner work to break free—no matter how unpleasant?

Go to a place where you can be alone and undisturbed for two to three hours. Take some blank sheets of paper or a blank notebook. Begin to write a letter to this person expressing your anger at what they did, how it felt, how you handled it at the time, and how you wish you had handled the situation. Don't hold back. If during the writing you want to yell, scream, beat a pillow, hit a tree with a stick, break something, DO IT! Just be sure you are alone and that no one else will interrupt you. Cry, scream, write, or verbalize as if you are speaking to the source of your anger. Remember to breathe!

Once you have completed the letter and the emotions are out, take several deep breaths. Now write again to this person.

Dear _____,

I release my need to be right in this situation. I want you to know that what I really want is approval and to be OK. I release my anger at you because it has held me captive long enough. I release any guilt for my anger. I forgive myself for holding on to this anger. I accept what you did was not intentional. I forgive you for not being the person I wanted you to be, for not doing the thing I wanted you to do, for not treating me the way I wanted to be treated. You are your own person, and I allow you to go your own way. I forgive you, and I forgive me. I realize that you are not here just to meet my needs, that you have your own needs, and that you are trying your best to do your best at this time. I am willing to use this forgiveness as an opportunity to grow my own self-worth and to grow in my awareness of how to handle my anger in the future so that I am able to be free and grow my relationship with others.

Thank you for allowing me to grow my life path skills.

Meditate and journal about this experience as the letter is never to be sent. It is your coaching and healing tool. Close your eyes and allow a release of the bond this anger has had on you. Breathe deeply for a minute or two. Bring the feeling of love into your heart. Take that feeling of love and picture the love surrounding the object of your anger. If you do not feel capable of this love after the letter, then ask your higher power to intervene and love this person until you can.

New Way to Handle Anger

1. Give yourself permission to feel angry, upset, and frustrated. Meditate, pray, or journal about it for a couple days. If the feeling is still there, it is a signal that something needs to be handled. Often a boundary has not been set or communicated, a need has not been identified, and an expectation has not been clearly explained.

2. Be sure you have taken time to think about your anger, upset, and/or frustration and that you choose an appropriate time to discuss it in a private place and with no time pressure.

3. Be willing to reframe your opinion of the situation or event. Be willing to suspend judgment toward the person.

4. State clearly your angry feelings:

   I am angry (upset, frustrated, irritated, disappointed, etc.) because:

   _____

   This makes me angry because: <u>(state results of actions or behaviors of the other person)</u>

5. Ask how the two of you can resolve the problem. Ask for what you want to happen. Ask them to state what they want to happen.

6. Be willing to release your need to have it "only your way" and to be "right"; be willing to listen to the other person. Stephen Covey says, "Seek first to understand, before being understood."

7. Be willing to set boundaries, make requests, and clearly state or clarify expectations. Realize that setting boundaries, asking for what you want, and stating clear expectations can cause frustration in other people. Accept the fact that you deserve to take care of yourself. You are responsible for setting boundaries. Others are not responsible for "mind reading" your boundaries or expectations.

8. Be willing to have these persons upset with you. You are responsible for taking care of your self-esteem and self-worth. You are responsible for your growth, not theirs!

9. Agree on each person's action

    You: I will _____

    Them: I will _____

    You have a choice. You can hold on to your old way of dealing with anger, and you can justify not growing through the uneasiness of a new way. Learning to handle anger allows you to become charmed. You take a giant step toward bringing your own energy and power into yourself rather than having it dissipated out to another person. Use your personal resolve to continue to handle your anger in new ways. Once you control anger, rather than anger controlling you, you have a powerful tool for coaching yourself along your life path.

FEAR

Fear is a personal experience. One person fears snakes while another enjoys having a snake as a pet. One person enjoys the thrill of public speaking, and another fears it so much that they freeze.

We have innate, natural fears to protect us from harm. Fear of falling is an example. Our body responds to fear with a sympathetic nervous system response to "flight or fight." Our brain is programmed to avoid danger. Think of a time you were driving and suddenly someone pulled out in front of you. You slammed on your brakes, and your body gave you a shot of adrenaline to help you respond with quick action and energy. Once the incident was over (and you didn't hit or get hit), there were a few moments where your heart raced and you took some shallow breaths, but then you took a deep breath and returned to the drive.

In daily life there are few life-threatening dangers, yet we still have fears. Stress is a form of fear in daily life—stress over bills, employees, bosses, children, and a myriad of other life situations. Fear in the form of stress keeps our body in a constant up and down of "fight or flight." Adrenaline rushes in and uses the body's energy in nonproductive ways. Stress triggers negative habits: sugar addiction, caffeine addiction, smoking, alcohol, exercise addiction, mental escapes, future focus, past focus, food addictions, buying addictions, and others.

Fear leaves you feeling powerless. The thing, person, and/or situation you fear holds power over you, your thoughts, and your actions. When you feel powerless, when you fear, you often look for something you can do to ease or block out the stress or fear. Thus, the negative habits listed above. Sometimes, the fear drives you to excessive attempts to control others, to take responsibility for others, to take care of others, or to rescue others. Conversely, fear can lead to inaction—being frozen or stuck.

Fear Worksheet

List the things you currently fear:

Samples: Failing at something;

... not doing _____ right

... being hurt by others

... hurting others' feelings

... debt

... not having enough _____

... change

... rejection

... "what others think"

... disappointing parents, spouse, children

... not being perfect enough

... losing my youth

... taking time off

... _____.

List any other specific fears you have about your job security, your family, your health, your income, and your future. What is fear costing you? Are you willing to take responsibility for changing your current fear/stress pattern? What would you gain if you could release some of these fears/stresses?

Breaking through fear's barrier takes a willingness to risk and to change. The risk to conquer fear and stress is to stretch your comfort zone. Comfort zones are a creation of your B.S., your belief system.

Go back to your list of fears and begin to walk into each one with a changed perception. Take one per week to conquer.

> "Resolve to do the things you fear and the death of fear is certain."
>
> Mark Twain

Write out the positive outcome that would dispel the fear. Take the positive statement, an affirmation, and read it every morning when you wake and before retiring.

For example:

Fear: I am afraid I will not have enough money to pay for school.

Affirmation: I am capable of finding new ways to increase my income.

> Action Cures Fear

Action: Resolve to learn more about scholarships for school or part-time, flexible income opportunities.

Affirming what you want is a process of reprogramming your B.S. It takes consistency and repetition. (See the chapter with the Affirmation Worksheet.) The B.S. you own is as old as you are. It took your whole life to create it. It will take some work to flush and refill your subconscious mind.

Lastly, read Susan Jeffers' book *Feel the Fear and Do It Anyway*. It was a life changer for me.

WORRY

Worry is negative prayer and negative visioning. As you worry, you create a negative impulse in your subconscious. Worry saps your energy because of its negativity. Also, worry keeps you either future focused, worrying what will happen, or past focused, worrying about what happened. Worry builds walls between people. While you are in a worry mode, you cannot be 100 percent present. For example, if you are worried about having enough money to pay the rent, you cannot really hear the concerns of your customers, coworkers, or your family. Worry contributes to low self-esteem. Worriers are convinced something negative will happen, and it keeps their self-esteem low and saps their energy. Think of Eeyore from Winnie-the-Pooh.

Take worry and turn it around. Put your mental focus on what you *do* want to happen in the situation. Mentally picture a positive outcome. Keep your focus there, and find out what action you can take to move toward what you want.

Worry-Busting Tool

1. List the people, places, and things that are on your current worry list.

2. List why you are worried about each person, place, and thing.

3. How does that worry affect you now?

4. What is the absolute worst thing that could happen if your worry came true? What would be the best thing that could happen?

5. What actions could you take **today** to change the negative outcome you are worrying about?

> Faith and Action cure worry.

Each worry-busting action you take empowers you to take others. Do not stop, do not look back—and don't feel guilty because you are not worrying.

If there is no action you can take, then overcome your worry with your faith in a higher power. LET IT GO. It is not yours to solve, fix, or change. "Faith" is the one power against which worry cannot stand, says Norman Vincent Peale in *The Power of Positive Thinking*. Find a copy of the Serenity Prayer, and repeat it aloud every morning and every evening. Give your worries to God, and get back into your life full force.

Once you add the three ways to handle any major dementors, you are ready to make great strides along your life path. People are their happiest when they are gripped in the throes of achievement and accomplishment.

Minor dementors: Compromise, Sin of Silence, Distractions

There are several other dementors that I have met along my life path.

Compromise. I call this "settling." When you convince yourself that you really are OK in this job, in this relationship, in this town, etc., are you settling? Do you tell yourself that changing would be too much, too hard, too costly, or too _____? Compromise is subtle and enticing because it is where most of the world lives, sitting on their potential like a couch potato. Not only do they sit there, but they would like nothing better than to have you stay on the couch with them (more about this in the section called "THEY"). It takes guts to own up to your own potential and get off the couch and out of compromise.

How do you know you are in compromise? Life feels like a drag. You see yourself in repeated patterns in daily life that you know you don't want and don't like, and that don't work. You want something better, yet you convince yourself it would just be too much work, or that it would upset those around you if you made the change that is burning in your soul.

In your life path, when you clarify your "on-fire" purpose, you will gather the guts to shake off compromise. Your purpose is the fuel to sustain your journey. Make one step toward your charmed life. Take the tools you have learned in this book and put them in your backpack. Put the backpack on your back and head out for the life of your dreams.

Two other dementors are **distractions** and **the Sin of Silence.** I am an expert at distractions because I am a recovering workaholic. I am a master of creating distractions to keep me from my next step or from facing something that might be uncomfortable. I can find all sorts of projects to keep me off my path. I can clean out closets, go shopping, or get lost in an unrelated project. But, I have also learned from my coaches to ask myself this question:

Is what I am doing taking me forward into my potential, toward my goals, or is it not?

The "Sin of Silence"

The opposite of anger is not speaking up, keeping silent to preserve peace and harmony, not asking for what you want. The "Sin of Silence" is the process of stuffing your own desires, your own goals, and your own potential to keep others from being uncomfortable with your new choices. It is easy to stuff feelings of frustration or even upsets when you OVER care about them and underserve yourself.

Maybe you were told, as I was, that disagreeing is not "OK" and that if you can't say something nice, don't say anything. It took a lot of reading, classes, and coaching for me to overcome this dementor in my life. Women, particularly women from the South, are taught to be nice.

How can you grow through this to be able to communicate your needs or boundaries to others, especially those close to you? You can use the Courageous Conversation Model that I have included. However, you may need preparation before using the model. I suggest two types of courses or online training: assertiveness and conflict management. I have benefitted from both, especially my first course in assertiveness. I came away a different person.

Here is the model if you are ready:

Courageous Conversation Model

Address tough issues with courage, compassion, and skill.

1. Name the issue.

2. Select a specific example that illustrates the behavior or situation you want to change or discuss.

3. Describe your feelings about the issue. Feelings are important in this step.

4. Clarify what is at stake. List the consequences if the situation does not change, including why you want this change.

5. Identify your part or your contribution to the situation. Maybe you have not spoken up before now; you have been silent. (NO one is innocent.)

6. Indicate that you want to resolve the issue and make this change. Acknowledge the value the other person holds for you.

7. Invite the other person to respond. Seek a dialogue to come to a full understanding. ("Dialogue" here means two or more people moving through meaning.)

8. Discuss what the two of you have learned and what is needed from each of you to resolve the issue, to make the change.

9. Agree what each party will do to resolve the issue or make the change. Determine how each of you will hold the other accountable for keeping the resolution.

You have now learned to handle your dementors. You can speak up for yourself; you can handle fear, anger and worry; and you can recognize and deal with compromise and distractions. You may need to revisit this chapter as you move along your life path. As I have learned, it is not a direct route. There are relapses and setbacks. However, your resolve to have a charmed life will keep you moving forward. There is no stopping your ability to grow the life of your dreams.

Chapter 8

Are you ready to walk an unknown path?

Chapter 8

Are you ready to walk an unknown path?

Your life path has perhaps been the same ole, same ole, and you are bored or frustrated with it all. Your life path may have been on one track, and now you want more or something different. Your life path may have gotten halted or altered, and you are struggling with a new path. For some reason, you are facing a new path, an unchartered, unknown path. You have made a new choice, and it is unfamiliar and maybe even scary.

Ego Drag

Something happens when you make new choices—your old ego creates drag on the new path. Your ego gets stuck in your past life, who it defines for you as "I." At times your ego will not be your friend. You will need to redefine "I" for your new SELF. That's scary because it is unknown and unfamiliar to you. If you have allowed others to define you, you will struggle until you get into your new SELF.

The *Urban Dictionary* defines "ego" this way:

The part of you that defines itself as a personality, separates itself from the outside world, and considers itself (read: you) a separate entity from the rest of nature and the cosmos. Perhaps necessary for survival in some evolutionary bygone, in modern times it leads only to (albeit often disguised) misanthropic beliefs and delusion. In short, "I." Ego is responsible for hate, fear, and delusion.

Think of your ego's old self-definition of "I" as being in SPANX®. You squeezed your being into a shape to please others or to even please your ego, but the squeeze cut off your life force. If you have ever worn SPANX®, you know that you can hardly breathe once you wiggle into the shape that is predetermined by the SPANX®. Moving into your new path will feel a bit messy, and there will be times you will wonder what the heck you are doing, trying to be someone you are not.

Time to journal

"I am" and what follows is how you define YOU. Ask yourself how you define "I am." Write out all the roles that your old "I" has defined as you. Write as many pages as it takes to define your current "I" roles. While you are in there poking at this sleeping giant, this ego, begin to journal, asking yourself the Dr. Phil question, "How is that working for you?"

Here is a list to get you started: Write your "I" statement for each.

- ✓ Career choice (for example, "I am a doctor.")
- ✓ Spouse/partner
- ✓ Mother/father
- ✓ Sibling
- ✓ Daughter/son
- ✓ Community/civic volunteer
- ✓ Church/synagogue participant
- ✓ Fitness/health level
- ✓ Prosperity level
- ✓ Culture of your upbringing
- ✓ Other role you have picked up along the way

> "The unexamined life is not worth living."
>
> Socrates

Journaling enables you to examine your role definitions. You bring your ego definition of YOU into the light of day. So often, we gather role expectations like a snowball rolling down the hill. We are unaware that we, at our soul level, never really wanted that role or that we never wanted that role "that way."

Once you have spent time journaling and reflecting, the next step is to meditate in order to remove or at least modify the influence of the old ego.

Your inner critic

The ego will rise like a phoenix from the flames in new forms. Those who are breaking away from an old role will run smack into their inner critic. The inner critic screams or whispers in your ear:

- You are not ready to make this change.
- You are not prepared to take on this new role.
- You don't have this new role down perfectly.
- You don't know how to do the new role PERFECTLY yet.
- You will embarrass yourself.
- They will think you are a bitch.

On and on the little voice goes.

The inner critic holds a high expectation for your performance in your new role. That high expectation is a hurdle you can conquer. It is just your ego trying to tame you back into those SPANX®. The recognition of what is happening with the voice of the ego is half of conquering the ego's voice in your head.

Visit me online for a meditation to help you let go of your inner critic. www.lifepathbydesign.net

Treasure Mapping

The treasure map process is a tool to expand your thinking and vision into new directions. I first learned about treasure mapping from Terry Cole Whitaker (see Resources). A treasure map feeds your mind new visual images and gets you out of your logical mind and into your creative mind. It brings fun and creativity into the process of re-birthing yourself along your life path.

Mary Katherine MacDougall says a treasure map represents "pictured prayer." Just as you would look at a map, or today a GPS app, to help you go from one place to another, a treasure map is a tangible picture of what you want to BE, to DO, or to HAVE.

Step 1 – Gather your materials. You can make this a wine and cheese event at your home with a few close friends, or you can do it alone. You'll need:

- ❑ Poster board or felt – cut to any size or shape you like. You can make this to hang on the wall or to fit in a notebook. I have done this on a retreat and we used felt so that the treasure map could be rolled up to go home in a suitcase. I cut the felt to the size of a standard poster board schoolchildren use.
- ❑ Glue and scissors – Yes, you are going to cut and paste. Glue sticks work for the poster board, and there is felt glue if you are using felt. If you have craft scissors,

those work fine, but just plain scissors are all you need.

- ❑ Old magazines – travel, fashion, health, animals, spiritual, and personal interest magazines, such a motorcycles or bicycles, etc. Ask friends for some of their old magazines or ask people to bring them to the treasure mapping event at your home.

- ❑ Optional – colored paper, glitter sticks, old broken jewelry, play money, or other small items that can be easily glued onto the treasure map.

Step 2 – Cut first. The process is free form. There is no right way to do the treasure map. You look through the magazines to find pictures or words that represent your future life path vision. It can have one for your new vocation, for instance, or it can have areas for different areas of your life where you want more fulfillment. The three big area are usually health, wealth (career), and relationships. These big areas can take many specific forms, such as a new home, a new location, more friends, travel, etc. Each person will find their own inspiration in pictures.

Plan on several hours to experience this. Let the first time be casual conversation while looking through the magazines with your scissors at hand. Cut the pictures that call to you or that you find fascinating. Cut out words or phrases that speak about what you want to become a part of your life. Play with placement once you have a group of pictures and words.

Some people are inspired by different colors. You can use the chakra colors to represent spiritual colors. There is an excellent website to discover more about chakra colors in the Resources section at the back of this book. In her book, *What Treasure Mapping Can Do for You*, Mary Katherine MacDougall gives these color suggestions:

Pink for health

Red for love

Green and gold for wealth and prosperity

Orange for energy

Sky blue or yellow for spiritual unfoldment

Lavender for service

Free form is just that. Go with colors that excite or inspire you, and then give the colors meaning yourself.

Step 3 – Paste away to make your treasure map unique to your desires and vision at this moment. As you paste, add any of the optional items to give the treasure map dimension and pop. Write in glitter. Paste on play money or plastic coins. Add jewels or gems. This is your creative picture.

Step 4 – If you are in a group, share about what you have created.

Step 5 – Hang your treasure map in a spot where you can see it, and spend time visualizing your new path. You can take time with each item you have placed on your treasure map and meditate on that one picture. You can take items on your treasure map and journal about what it will be like when that is in your life. You can take items and write affirmations about the items or idea in your journal.

Ease on down the road

Your treasure map is your creative masterpiece that will open a window to your creative self that will help the unknown path you are on become real in your life. Your time spent creating a visual will ease you into trying on this new part of your life. Your new life path choice is there as a visual, and it becomes less unknown. You become at ease with your new life path by spending time with your creative self through your treasure map.

Getting unstuck

Stepping into the unknown is not always a direct path. One of the images that I have used in my consulting is this:

Frozen ⟹ Unfreeze ⟹ Refreeze

Think of your old life path as frozen solid like an ice cube. You embark to new places on your life path. You unfreeze. Water unfrozen is a puddle with no shape. This shapeless time feels weird, uncomfortable, and messy. Hang in there. Go with the "flow" as the saying goes. Be willing to experience this DIS-comfortable place as you lean into your new direction. You will soon be taking the training wheels off and be in a new frozen, a new normal.

People abandon new life path choices when this dis-comfortable feeling enters in and the ego talk draws you back toward the old SPANX®. Pushing through with faith (See section "Who ya gonna call?") and actions toward your new path is, in fact, the way to the other side.

When you feel stuck or like you want to run back to the old, find what is going to be your new tool or solution. Revisit your treasure map, and/or journal about your discomfort to see if there is a root cause. Find a coach, find a course, and find a book to support you in staying the course. When you get past your shapeless puddle, you will be stronger for any life path changes in your new future. Once you break free of your self-imposed SPANX®, you will never return to the old ego self. You are freeing your own soul to soar to new heights.

Chapter 9

Is it time for a walk?

Chapter 9

Is it time for a walk?

Got a challenge, got a problem, got a messy relationship issue, got no inspiration, or got that stuck feeling? It's time for a walk.

As you process and integrate the tools and new thoughts from this book, you may feel a bit overwhelmed, or you may need just to take a mental break to clear your mind. Over the years of getting my life back on path, rediscovering my path, and clearing the sticky relationship issues with either my children or my spouse, a good walk combined with either a paper or pencil or another person with whom I can talk things out is a good exercise to move forward, literally and figuratively.

Nature is where you reconnect with your essence. We are surrounded by buildings, and we live and work inside rooms that may not have an outdoor view. Nature is healing. Find a beach, a mountain path, a wooded lane, a lake, a stream, or a city park. Allow yourself time to turn off all electronics. This is not the time to wear ear buds with your iPod® playing. This is time to allow the sights, the sounds, or the silence be your environment.

The couple connection walk.

Do you have an issue with your partner? A walk is in order. Leave the kids, the emails, the dishes, and the other chores, and make your escape into nature. Find your own special walking place. Stone Mountain Park in Atlanta; the wetlands of St. Augustine, Florida; the beach anywhere have all been special places for relationship walk-talks for me. A walk in nature is the place to find your voice in the relationship situation that is your current challenge.

What do you want that is not present in the relationship? Define what you really want. Be honest with yourself first and then with your partner. This is not the place to spew blame or judgment. Neither of those allow you to mend the relationship. Taking responsibility for what you want is first. Often, you are just unhappy. It is hard for a partner to solve "unhappy" for you. And, in the world of relationships, it is not up to your partner to make you happy. Your responsibility is to define what you want and to be willing to ask for it. Do you need more time to be a loving couple, perhaps a date night? Do you need more help around the house?

Do you want more shared child care? Your job is to be definite about what you want. This may require an alone walk before the couple walk.

Once you can define what you want, and once you have asked for what you want, then it is time to listen. Be ready to listen—really listen, without waiting for your turn to defend or to make your point. Listening without jumping in can be one of the hardest things you will ever learn, AND it is one of the most important.

The process that I learned years ago is called active listening or reflective listening. You allow your partner to respond to your request, OR perhaps your partner has a request. You listen without judging or jumping in. You ask for clarification to be sure you understand. Then the two of you can dialogue (which means move through meaning) about the situation.

There is hardly a week that goes by that I do not have a walk-talk with my partner. Walking to talk things out is a relationship saver. Supportive relationships are important as you move along your life path. I would never have accomplished what I have without my partner's support.

> The couple that walks together, stays together.

Getting Unstuck Walk

Being stuck somewhere along your life path is never fun. However, the recognition that you are stuck is awesome insight. Through awareness, you can now get unstuck. Often, a good long walk with your journal is the answer. Go to a place that inspires you. Find your own spot to sit and just be in thankfulness for the nature that surrounds you. Use your pad and pen to write down all the things for which you are thankful or appreciative. Write at least twenty to thirty—more if they keep coming.

Just be in gratitude for what you have in your life.

> "All you need is deep within you waiting to unfold and reveal itself. All you have to do is be still and take time to seek for what is within and you shall surely find it."
>
> Eileen Caddy

Next, write at the top of a page:

Things I want to do – List at least twenty without any barriers or doubts. This is a dream list, and you don't want filters spoiling the inspiration of the process.

Next, top of a page:

Things I want to have – List at least twenty things that you do not currently possess that you want in your life, from a simple massage to a house on the beach. Dream without filters or how-tos.

Next, top of the page write:

Who I want to be – List at least twenty things you want to be in your life. For example, you might want to be more articulate, more outgoing, more courageous, more social, or more spiritual.

Before the next page, lay down your pen and pad and close your eyes. Take several deep breaths to center your mind. Let your mind drift to some of the things that stand out from your lists. Visualize yourself doing something from your first list. See your body as you engage in this activity. See who is with you or if you are alone in doing this. Notice your feelings as you do something on your list. Anchor that feeling by putting your dominant hand's thumb and your middle together as you feel those feelings of doing that activity.

Next, visualize yourself having something from your next list. Visualize the place, the environment, and the colors. Hear the sounds. Smell the smells. Notice the feeling of having some item on your list. Anchor that feeling by putting your dominant hand's thumb and your middle finger together as you feel those feelings of having. Take a deep breath to center on that feeling with your fingers together.

Lastly, visualize yourself being the person on your last list. See yourself in your mind's eye being as you want to be. Listen to yourself and feel how you are feeling being this. Anchor this being feeling by placing your dominant hand's thumb and your middle finger together as you feel the feeling.

Take several cleansing breaths, come back to your special place, and pick up your pen and pad. Journal about what you now see as a possible future for yourself. Once you have journaled, look over your lists and your journal pages. Center on two to three steps—not leaps, mind you, steps—that you want to take to move on your life path toward something new, something more, or something different.

Use this special place and the exercise anytime you are down or stuck, or when you need some new inspiration.

The family walk

Walking with your children is a powerful way to connect, reconnect, stay in touch, or problem solve. There have been many walks with my two sons in my life as a mom, but one stands out.

> Remember: The walk is unplugged.

My younger son, Greg, had graduated from high school in Tampa, Florida, where he was living with his dad. His dad had promised a cross-country trip after graduation, so Greg had not applied to college. He thought he would take a year off to travel with his dad. Mid-summer after graduation, he found out that the road trip was off. He piled in his car and came to stay with my husband and me. To say he was a lost puppy is an understatement. Greg had been in the gifted program at school since the fifth grade and had a scholarship to go to a Florida college tuition-free through the Florida Academic Scholar Program.

At that time, I was newly remarried. My husband and I were living in Atlanta, Georgia. My heart was torn for Greg, and yet I knew I was just getting accustomed to being remarried. It was time for a walk/talk. Greg and

I drove to Stone Mountain Park near where we lived. A lovely part of the park, Indian Island, is located just across a relocated covered bridge. Greg and I walked around the island once, just talking about possible futures for him. He was concerned about getting into a college this late.

Adult children returning home can be a blessing or it can be a nightmare. My husband and I have four children between us. In our pre-marriage conversations, we agreed that we would support each of the four through their bachelor's degrees. After they each earned their bachelor's, they would be on their own. My husband would assist and support his two children, and I would support my two.

I have seen the return of adult children tear families apart, divide spouses, and generally wreak havoc because the parents (or one parent) will not set boundaries. My spouse and I wanted to avoid those issues. Our boundaries were these: as long as the son or daughter was a full-time student in their bachelor's studies, we would support them totally. If they were not a full-time student, they could live with us rent-free for three months while contributing to household chores. After three months, they were expected to contribute a fair share to rent and household expenses.

As Greg and I walked Indian Island, I communicated those guidelines to him. He understood that while he lived with us we would expect him to share in chores and be accountable for his whereabouts. He could stay with us until he could figure things out for his life. Our request was for him to let us know if he was not coming home so that we would not worry. He was asked to call us before 11:00 p.m. to let us know. He was a high school graduate, so there was no curfew—just the courtesy call if he was not coming home. We agreed to pay his car insurance and gas money during those three months until he sorted his own life path out.

Though he was disappointed with his situation, he took responsibility for staying within the boundaries that we set for him. He first got a job delivering pizzas. Next, he checked into enrolling into the local junior college. He was just under the wire to enroll and start classes in the fall.

That walk is forever in my memory. As parents, you will not know the reaction your children will have when you set boundaries. You need your own center to take care of yourself and your spouse. If you fear that the son or daughter will leave and never come back, you will not set appropriate boundaries. That leaves you vulnerable to some of the unfortunate situations that friends have let happen with their adult children. Remember: you are the senior adult AND you deserve a life. Your adult children need to find their own path, even if it is not the one you would want for them. They have to skin their own knees and solve some of their own problems. Playing rescuer leads to dependency and resentment.

A walk as self-care and re-connection to your source

Walking in nature is one self-care routine that serves me well. The awe of nature is always soul nourishing. Sharing that experience with my family is very special. The alone walks are nourishing also. God created the vast world of nature, and God created you. You and God together in nature's setting can work together to create a charmed life and solve any challenges.

Chapter 10

Do you have the energy you need for your life path?

Chapter 10

Do you have the energy you need for your life path?

I slumped to the floor, sliding my back against the door of his office that kept me from falling. I was in my business suit, hose, and heels. I had hit the wall and was seeking help. Exhaustion is not your friend when you are trying to accomplish big goals.

He asked me to follow him. I walked to the back of his office where he had a fully equipped gym. He asked me to get on the stationary bike and pedal for thirty minutes. I made it for four minutes. With a bit of Jewish-mother guilt, he admonished me for letting myself get into such poor shape. He then TOLD—not asked—me to meet him at six o'clock the next morning at the gym to begin the journey back to health.

That day in 1998, Dr. Jay Hammer began the process of coaching me back to health. I showed up at six o'clock that next morning, and he coached me through a workout that I still use today. He gave me diet guidelines. I got my life and my energy back.

Sometimes you need to break down to build up. Sometimes you need a voice of reason. One of my trainers, Diane, recently had said to me, "Miss Linda, you need to take better care of yourself if you are going to build this business like you are saying." You come to the place of knowing that self-care is a critical part of leading a charmed life.

What is self-care?

Self-care consist of rituals or activities that enable you to take care of your body, soul, and spirit regularly. Self-care provides the stamina and the energy you need to lead a charmed life.

Elements of self-care include food choices, exercise, therapeutic massage, meditation time, time on your own, and other pursuits that bring you joy. Only *you* know what nourishes *you*. Yet if you are stressed or unhappy, you may have buried what you really need. Take a journey with me as I ask you about self-care components, and ask yourself what would make you feel alive and energized.

What food choices work for YOU?

Over my life I have tried a myriad of diets. (Maybe you have too?) From Atkins in the '80s to gluten-free today. I function best with high protein, low carb, and gluten free food choices. Because I live in the beautiful state of California, I have an abundance of fresh organic vegetables available all year. I love to cook and shop for fresh vegetables and fruits, so I make it a priority to seek those for my food choices.

You will need to find what works for you. In the Resources section, several books are listed that can help you learn about food choices that can give you the energy and vitality that your life path needs. In my experience, you need to find that out for yourself. What works for your coworkers or mom or sister may or may not work for you. Also, do not require everyone in the house to follow your lead. You can ask, but it is not a requirement. As my husband has often said, "What are WE eating this week?" He has been a trooper and has followed along with a few things I have experimented with, but not all. I respect his choice not to follow MY food choices.

What is your best food choice routine? There is no need to become a food Nazi; it turns people off. Take responsibility for what you need. For example, I travel with a small blender to make my protein shake in my room, rather than be seduced by the FREE, bad choices at the breakfast bar.

What exercise makes you happy?

There is no doubt that regular exercise is essential to your energy your brain health and well-being along your life path. Find what you love and what you will do consistently. I like variety. I try to be at the gym for aerobic exercise with the elliptical for thirty minutes and then a free-weight routine from Dr. Jay two to three days per week. I like to ride my bicycle for several miles at least once per week. I go to a yoga class once per week. And I always want a beach walk at least once per week. But hey, that is my charmed life exercise routine. What will yours include?

One hundred fifty minutes per week of aerobic exercise is the BAM (bare-ass minimum). What do you want to do to accomplish your BAM? Jazz dancing, swimming, roller blading, jogging, walking, bicycling, or gymnasium visits? Whatever you choose, be sure it has portability if you travel. I got into trouble not exercising when I traveled for client visits. At the peak of my business, I traveled a lot. I learned to carry my workout clothes and hit the hotel gym at 5:45 a.m. to ensure exercise happened.

Look for ways you can incorporate exercise into your family weekend lifestyle. When Ted and I lived in Stone Mountain, Georgia, we routinely hiked the five-mile trek around the mountain on weekends. In St. Augustine, Florida, we would take long bike rides on the flat terrain. Here in California, we walk the beach or find a mountain trail to hike on most weekends. For me, an outdoor activity every week is soul nourishing and a part of my charmed life.

What outdoor activity would you chose? Road biking, kayaking, skiing? There are a number of varied outdoor activities.

> Just Get Out There

Energizing extras

Therapeutic massage, sauna visits, or steam baths can add to your self-care routine. All have health benefits, and you can add one or all into your life. The point with the extras is that you will need to clarify for yourself, like L'Oréal says:

> You are WORTH it!

Where does the time and money for self-care come in?

Budgeting money and time for self-care is part of making your way to a charmed life. If everyone else in your life comes first, you will run out of energy to take care of them. Start by adding a self-care element into your week, or twice per month. Starting is half-done. Self-care is worth the conversation you may need to have with your partner or your children. Children have a higher respect for you if you are able to articulate to them that you take care of yourself so that you can take care of them. If you are the sacrificial person who gives up your own desires to care for your partner and children, then you will get lost, they will become dependent on your sacrifice, and in the long run they may not even appreciate your sacrifice.

Chapter 11

How do you relate to your partner along your evolving life path?

Chapter 11

How do you relate to your partner along your evolving life path?

This book is about you. You do have to define and create the life path that satisfies your soul, yet most of us want a significant other to walk the path with us. At times this can be tricky, especially as you grow and change. Read on and add another tool to your coaching backpack.

From "Lollipop" to Real

Two couples got my attention as I rode the Wally Park garage shuttle to Los Angeles airport at a quarter till six one morning. One middle-aged couple sat across from me. She was a well-dressed blond with a felt hat in her hands. Her partner wore a polo shirt and had short-cropped hair with light gray at his temples. She asked a question I could not hear but he snipped a reply that bothered her. She put the hat over her face. He made a comment about that, and as she moved the hat, tears rolled down her cheeks. He said, "Not this again," and turned away in disgust.

On the backseat of the same 5:45 a.m. shuttle was a millennial couple going over their travel papers. They giggled and cooed at each other. He turned to her and tapped his finger on his cheek, silently asking for a kiss. She beamed at the request and planted a loving kiss on his cheek.

How do couples go from giggly passion to disgust? I thought. How can we keep our own personal passion for life while in a relationship? How do we manage to keep the positive energy ahead of the drama and the conflict in our significant relationships?

It brought to mind a talk I heard while I was in Atlanta attending a post-divorce singles group. The minister said that early in a new relationship we live in a dream world she called "lollipopville." We are so physically attracted that the hormones rush in to cloud our judgment.

Then we move in with our lover who leaves the cap off the toothpaste. We get married and find out that our mate is a neat freak. We are in phase two of a relationship with another person. The tricky phase.

We enter the early phase of human relationships with high expectations. We set an ideal in our mind about how this person will fulfill our expectations and dreams. Those expectations have been unspoken because we were in the early fragile phase. We want the other person to fulfill our dreams and desires and not run away before the relationship has a chance. We don't want to drive them away with any requests or critiques, so we say nothing or we beat around the proverbial bush.

Is there a better way to move from "lollipop" to real? YES. I also believe it is an ongoing process to debug our intimate human relationships. (I say "human" because if your dog disappoints you, you can take it to obedience training. I have not seen obedience training for our human companions.)

Debugging your intimate relationships can require two tools. One tool is the "Sunday meeting", which I will explain. The other tool is debugging yourself. Since much of what upsets us is our own mental yardstick, our pre-programmed high expectations of what behavior is OK and what is not OK. We can often get the relationship back on track with some internal tweaking.

"Sunday meeting"

What is a "Sunday meeting" you ask? My husband and I are marriage second-timers. Previously, he was married seventeen years, and I was married twenty years. I felt that our new marriage needed some preventions in place to ensure that this second marriage for both of us had a chance to become a long-lasting relationship. Sylvia, my life coach, taught us about "Sunday meeting." The process is simple but not always easy. She asked us to find a time each week (our time was on Sunday after church, thus Sunday meeting) to sit down and look back over the past week and look forward and into the upcoming week. We were to ask each other, in turn, three questions:

What's working?

What's not working?

Are there any requests?

What's working?

Set aside uninterrupted time to talk with your partner. Start with communicating "What's Working?" Each person in turn acknowledges to the other the things that they have done that have pleased us. Couples can easily fall into taking each other for granted, and as is often the case, we have different expectations about acknowledging our love. You'll recall the old story about the older couple. She turns to him and says, "Honey, you never tell me you love me." Her spouse replies, "I told you 'I love you' when we got married. I'll let you know if anything changes."

Two people are attracted to each other for the difference in their styles. One partner is often a gabby gusher, effusing emotion and showing love verbally and physically. The other might be quiet and reflective, reluctant to show affection, especially in public. The "Sunday meeting" is a specific time to let the other person know how they have pleased us during the week. This gives us clues about how the other person likes to be shown the love we have for them. We are different in our love language. If you only show love the way you want to be shown love, you may miss the mark.

What's not working?

This exchange is where the rubber meets the road in developing a REAL relationship and deepening love. I lived in a first marriage where we never spoke harshly, we never yelled, we never complained to each other. We lived in a false glass bubble of "We're doing fine." I grew up in a family that did not tolerate conflict and that was harsh with punishment if you disagreed with a parent. Our family put on a happy face to the world, so I never learned to deal with conflict. I did not know how to approach someone and tell the truth about my concerns or frustrations. I learned to bury all that and keep silent. Therefore, this process was difficult but oh, so necessary for Ted and me to develop a REAL relationship.

It not only takes guts to tell the truth about your feelings when your love does or says something that is hurtful, or when they forget something, it also takes guts to hear the things that bother your lover. Because it is a two-way street, you can help each other through the tough spots. The agreement is that you will stay present to discuss, but not justify, defend, or blame; those three retorts take you nowhere. Both partners will need an open heart and a willingness to take responsibility for their actions or inactions. We have to be willing to allow the other person to have the feelings they have about what we have done or have not done.

Forgiveness is crucial to this process also. In a love relationship, our partner does not purposefully do or not do or say something. Most of the time we are creatures of habit, and we are not always thinking through what we are doing. Now that we are in a relationship with another, we have to become conscious of how our behaviors affect our lover. Forgive the other, take the information, and work to modify behaviors that are pesky to our lover.

However, there are limits to what we can or should do to please another. We are not asking for full-on character changes. We are asking for modifications that will smooth out our frustrations with each other. My strong, silent mate will not need to become a jabber mouth to please me. Yet if I am the jabberwocky, I can learn (as I have) that first thing in the morning is not the best time to have a conversation with him. I wake up ready to go headlong into my day. He, on the other hand, takes a few hours to allow the day to take hold. We've learned to have meaningful conversations at lunch or dinner or with a mid-morning walk at the beach.

Through our "Sunday meetings", I learned that when I do have an upset that has gone to strong emotions within me, I should NOT throw the emotions out there in RAW. (RAW is the photography term that indicates there has been no Photoshop® editing done to the photograph; it is RAW.) My spouse cannot hear anything I say through strong emotions. I have learned to meditate, journal, and take a walk around the block in my mind to sort through my emotions to get to the underlying issue. I then look at my part in the issue and take responsibility for that. When an issue has had time to mature and not be RAW, then I will ask for a "Sunday Meeting."

Requests?

The last part of the "Sunday meeting" is to ask each other if there are any requests for the upcoming week, anything special that either would like to do or anyplace special that either would like to go. End with a hug and go back into your day or evening.

"Sunday meetings" are great to combine with a walk. The "Sunday meeting" tool is always there for us to use. We know we can ask each other for a "Sunday meeting" to help us navigate through the sticky issues that will come up in a relationship.

Debugging yourself

Any relationship can hit eddies or shoals of life and create frustration and unease—that walking-on-eggshells feeling. There are times that this unease is about you and not about them. Unfortunately, as Zig Ziglar says in his kick the Cat story (this is my paraphrase): *When you have a bad day at work and those issues do not get resolved, you can often come home and kick the cat.* We can come home from a bad day, a bad week, feeling frustrated about our job or children, and dump those frustrations on the one we love. We project onto our loved one that the problem is something that they are doing or not doing.

Hold your horses, put the brakes on, and get time with yourself to really look at your upset with your partner. My favorite teacher on this topic is Byron Katie (see Resources). She asks you to query yourself with three questions:

1. Is it true?

2. Can you absolutely know that it is true?

3. How do you react? What happens when you believe that thought?

4. Who would you be without the thought?

These seem simple, but they are not. Katie's questions make you look inside at the story you are telling yourself about the situation. She asks that you "get real" about the story. We are very competent at cooking up stories in our head. We feed the story to our self as if it is true without ever really checking it out OR looking to see what filter we are using to think that way.

The next time you want to lash out at your partner, STOP, take a deep breath, and go inside yourself first. Ask yourself this question: What is it that I want, that I am not getting right now? Is it my partner's job to give it to me? Louise Hay, another of my favorite authors and teachers, says you must first love yourself before you can be in a healthy relationship with another. The first relationship to get in shipshape is your relationship with yourself. That is a life path journey.

Chapter 12

Who ya gonna call?

Chapter 12

Who ya gonna call?

The movie *Ghostbusters* gave us that memorable phrase: "Who ya gonna call?" When you need to get unstuck, to find a direction, to get through the messy frustration of change, or perhaps to talk it all out before you launch into a new direction, a coach can be the one to call. Or, there may be a book or a CD that can help you along your way. Call on God. Connect or reconnect with your source, your God, your spiritual nature. Your readiness will draw to you the next guide for your life path.

> When the student is ready, the teacher will appear.

Coaches

Coaches have helped me design and live my own charmed life. One coach helped me see that I needed a new path. One coach helped me get past the anger that was consuming me after my divorce. One coach helped my husband and me get back on our loving path. One coach helped me move to a new phase in my life, including a discovery to write this book.

Life coaching is a relationship between you and the coach that enhances your life fulfillment. A life coach can help you discover new paths, reclaim lost parts of yourself, help you set the goals that will move you along, help you clarify your life purpose, and help you overcome stones, dementors, and roadblocks in your path.

A coach can be someone with a specific method that you study. Bill Lamond was both. I met Bill when we were both speakers at a women's conference. At the time I was frustrated with my business, I was tired of traveling so much and I felt stuck within my business model.

Bill gave a two-day workshop that I attended, and then I asked if he would be my life coach. Through Bill, I was able to let go of many old patterns that had made me successful but were now barriers to a new type of life that I wanted. I'll never forget Bills' comment as I was whining about not being able to change. He wisely said, "Linda, that old working-hard model of life has served you well. Look at the success you have created. You are complete with that model though. It is time to

BE COMPLETE so that you can move into a different model of success."

As Bill coached me, I was able to let go of the workaholic Mini-me that had run my life. I was able to see the beauty of the business I had created, and then to see beyond that path to see new opportunities to live my charmed life with more time off and more time with my husband. It was not an easy process, but with Bill's guidance I was able to change. When I would whine that I only knew how to work hard, he was there to urge me on by asking me to live "as if" I knew how to engage in life without the workaholic Mini-me running things.

Coaches can come from a referral or a chance meeting at a personal development conference, or through a book you read where you found yourself resonating with the author. That's how I found Patrick Harbula. He wrote a book that was the topic of a class I attended at my church, *Magic of the Soul*. At that time, I was antsy to make some changes in my career path (again), and he offered a complimentary coaching session. His coaching and guidance led me to writing this book and to becoming a life coach.

Life coaching is a growing cottage industry. There are life coaches just about everywhere you turn. Find a life coach that you feel in your gut is good for your path NOW. Is there an initial session to get a "gut feel" for this coach and how you like them? This, to me, is paramount. You need to feel their acceptance and their support.

Google "life coach" in your area, or visit a few new thought churches or business organizations and you will meet life coaches. New thought churches are Unity, Centers for Spiritual Living, and Unitarian. Business organizations that attract life coaches are NAWBO (National Association of Women Business Owners), lead groups, chambers of commerce, etc.

Books and CDs

How can books or CDs alter your life path? My dementors and demons came to roost when I was suddenly uprooted from a home that I loved in Nashville, Tennessee. In Nashville, my two sons were in a good school, I worked as a dental hygienist for a really great dentist, and we had a lovely home. My husband decided to change jobs and move us to Charleston, South Carolina. While I waited to take the dental hygiene board exam, I got a bit lost in my own depression and hit the bottle of sherry a little too hard. My son can home from school one day and asked a life-changing question, "Mom, are you ever going to get out of your nightgown?" He got my attention.

Six months after we moved to South Carolina, my husband moved to Florida for another job. This was the beginning of the end of my marriage though I did not want to admit it. I was scared. My son's question forced me to "get a grip" and to look at my choices. My husband, who was in sales, had some motivational cassettes on the shelf. I started listening to those motivational cassettes all day. I flooded my mind with new ways of thinking, and I slowly began to look at life through a different portal. That was when I made the decision:

> If it is to be, it is up to me.

I began to cultivate my own potential rather than settling for being an extension of someone else.

I found those motivational cassettes so inspiring that I became a sales rep for the cassette production company, success Motivation Institute. On a sales call (by the way, I hated sales), the owner of a new franchise company asked me a life path changing question: she asked me if I would use the cassette program materials to train her new franchisees. I said "yes", without knowing one thing about training—except that I loved to go to seminars. Answering YES to that question changed my life path. Training was a new path, not sales.

That training position gave me a peek into my new life that I didn't even know about. At that time I just wanted to have an alternative career path from dental hygiene because I had to take a board exam for every state. Through a temporary job, I was introduced to a consulting firm that hired me to be a hygiene department trainer. I found a new life path that led to a successful career and ultimately my own business as a dental management consultant and speaker.

That was a time for me to "get real" with the life I was leading. Have you ever given up what you want to serve your children, your spouse, your mom, your uncle? You get the picture. This is where a tear in your **who-ness** comes into your life. You proceed to give up your possibilities to serve others. It seems like a good daughter, spouse, and mother idea at the time. Others' wants and needs come first one time, then another, and soon it becomes who you are. You are there to serve all but yourself; your needs are *last* or *lost*. You even lose touch with your own self in this game of life.

My turnaround came through reading and listening to those cassettes. Over and over and over again. In the cassette program that started my new path, Paul J. Meyer said that it took six repetitions of the same information for a person to BEGIN to own the information as true. Meyer believed in spaced repetition. His theory was that repeating the same information over a span of time would increase retention. Meyer used the advertising industry as the model. The first time you see or hear an ad, you may or may not even recognize it. The second time you see or hear the ad, it seems a bit familiar. The third time you see or hear the ad, you recognize it. The fourth time it is familiar. The fifth time you see or hear the ad, you know a few of the words. The sixth time you are singing along, or you know the words to the ad or the jingle.

Meyer's Success Motivation Institute became my rolling classroom and my turnaround. The first and foundational program is "The Dynamics of Personal Goal Setting." This ten-week course was a combination of a workbook, notebook, and ten cassettes. Those cassettes and that workbook showed me how to design my own life path.

Those ten lessons on ten cassettes were life changing. No one had ever sat me down and introduced me to my potential and my power to dream and have things happen on my terms. I went from being a depressed wife whining that my husband had not made me happy to learning to take my life, my happiness, and my potential back into my own hands.

To this day, I always have a business, motivational, or inspirational CD in my car. Now I have books on Audible® to play while I get my makeup on in the morning and while I drive from here to there. Before Audible®, it was CDs. I've listened to Tony Robbins and his series, *Unlimited Potential*, while putting on my make-up. Over, and over and over again.

On my night stand is a non-fiction personal improvement book and a fiction. I have *SUCCESS*, *Oprah's Magazine* and the *Science of Mind* magazine in the other reading room. The authors in Resources have been my way showers, my coaches and my motivation along the path.

Your job is to fortify not only your diet and your body, but to fortify your mind. Turn off the TV and the bad news or the drama and open your mind to the inspiration of the masters. I love what Wayne Dyer said about the news, "*If there is something bad enough that I need to know it, someone will tell me.*" I do not have to purposely listen or watch bad news."

GOD/Source

"Jesus wants me for a sunbeam" is a tune I recall singing as a child. My Southern Baptist upbringing gave me a firm resolve to have strong spiritual values. My path changed to Unity, a new thought church, after my divorce because at that time, the Southern Baptists were none too keen on divorce. Through Unity and now Center for Spiritual Living, I have found a wonderful acceptance and place for my spiritual life growth. I love that we accept all faiths, beliefs, and religions. I believe there are many paths to God, Source, Divine Mind, or whatever you name the spiritual existence in your life.

A charmed life will include finding or nurturing your spiritual source and seeking out a place to grow your spiritual self. Faith is the foundation to see you through all that your life path will bring, especially the dark times.

One of the best ways to connect with your spiritual self is through meditation. I have to say that learning the powerful process of meditation has made my life path ever so much easier, but I am a late bloomer with meditation. Over the years I have used guided meditation with authors such as Shakti Gawain, but I never really stopped to learn to meditate. One of the classes I took taught me how to meditate, and I have been a fan and practitioner ever since. The book that helped me really get the technique down is *The Joy of Meditation,* Jack and Cornelia Addington.

Your life path is awaiting you. Your charmed life is calling. This book offers you many tools, exercises, and meditations to assist you in growing your own potential and becoming your own coach. Life Path by Design is in your court now. It is your access to, as the Army says, "Be all you can be."

ETC. – Epilogue

Change is messy. Change is uncomfortable. That's why they call it leaving your comfort zone. Change is something that you do for a baby's diaper, and even they protest the change at times. Learning to navigate change is your ticket to a charmed life.

This book has provided a dozen or more tools for your journey along your life path, but reading the book will not make your life charmed. Only you can do that.

Your mind will produce excuses not to change. You will not need anyone outside your own Mini-me mind. Change gets messy because Mini-me will convince you that the excuses that come up are real. Learn to recognize the voice of your Mini-me, your ego, or your dementors. Learn to halt these in their tracks:

Change will be difficult.

Change will be risky.

I am not ready to try.

There will be huge family drama.

I don't deserve it.

It's impossible.

I am really OK.

What am I thinking?

It is not my nature.

I can't afford it.

This is impractical.

No one will help me.

It has never happened before.

I am not strong enough.

I am not smart enough.

The rules won't let me.

I don't have the energy.

I am too busy.

I am scared.

I have a good paycheck where I am.

I don't really need anything else.

I am content; my life is fine where I am.

    The reality is that the path to a charmed life is not a straight shot. There will be change and challenges to continue on your path. You will be in constant creation and re-creation of your charmed life. As you grow your potential, your horizons will broaden. Life is full of possibilities if you are willing to coach yourself to your own charmed life. Call me if you need or want coaching along the way. 800.242.7648

In Appreciation...

This book would not have been possible without the love and support of my dear husband, Ted Mathews. Ted has allowed me to explore, to fall on my face, to dream, to make mistakes, to work overtime again and again, to be gone for extended periods to explore personal growth courses and retreats, to expand my horizons, and to cry on his shoulder—all the while loving me and trusting in our relationship. His allowing and his support of my Life Path by Design has led us both into charmed lives. We have explored the world together, walked mountain trails and along the beach. Life is better hand in hand with Ted. Thank you for loving me.

To my mentors ...

Sylvia Sultenfuss, Bill Lamond, Patrick Harbula, and the supportive team of AVATAR Masters have each in their own special way opened doors, opened my mind and my heart, and have been way-showers along my path. Dr. Kennedy Schultz, Reverend Carol O'Connell, Reverend Ken Wilcox, and Reverend Bonnie Rose, along with Unity and Centers for Spiritual Living ministers over thirty years of study have brought me to a close relationship with my spiritual source. My spiritual growth has been a catalyst all along my life path. Without their ongoing inspiration and thought-provoking ministry, I would never have written this book.

To my sons ...

WOW, I could not be prouder of the men you are. Greg, you dove into your life path head and heart first. Your triumphs and struggles have taught me and allowed me to see your strength, as well as your tender heart. Paul, your miracle turnaround has touched my heart and soul many times. You have forged your own unique life path with wisdom, drive, and fortitude. You are a poster child for doing it your own way. You both have given me such delight in being your MOM. I would not have missed that part of my life path for anything.

To my left-turn inspiration ...

Paul J. Meyer, though you have moved on to another plane, your personal development programs started my journey on a totally new life path. Who knew all the things that would be possible in my life when I listened again and again and again and again to your cassettes and worked the workbook from Success Motivation Institute? Your inspiration through your materials changed my life, and I am forever grateful.

About Linda Drevenstedt

"Cultivating Potential in People"

Linda Drevenstedt nurtures, explores, and seeks life's "aha" moments to challenge her coaching clients to cultivate their potential. For over twenty years, Linda has run a highly successful consulting firm. Her Steel Magnolia wit and wisdom has helped her coaching clients move through barriers to great success.

Before starting her own consulting and coaching business, she was a dental hygienist and a dental practice administrator. Her background also includes a master's degree in health care administration and a bachelor's in business management. She studied life coaching with Patrick Harbula.

Linda has coauthored two books and is the author of *Life Path by Design*, published on Amazon.com.

When Linda coaches or speaks, people have "aha" moments of their own and take home practical action steps to cultivate more potential in their lives.

Connect with Linda

Website:	www.lifepathbydesign.net
Email:	linda@lifepathbydesign.net
Facebook:	https://www.facebook.com/LifePathByDesign
Twitter:	@ldrevenstedt
LinkedIn:	http://www.linkedin.com/pub/linda-drevenstedt/a/6aa/ba4
Mailing Address:	11314 Beechnut Street; Ventura, CA 93004
Phone:	800.242.7648

Resources for Life Path by Design

To help you with your vision:

The 8th Habit by Stephen Covey

Acres of Diamonds by Russell Corwell

The Magic of the Soul by Patrick Harbula

The Magic of Thinking Big by Claude Bristol

The Power of Purpose by Richard Leider

The Seven Habits of Highly Effective People by Stephen Covey

The Seven Spiritual Laws of Success by Deepak Chopra

Think and Grow Rich by Napoleon Hill

Unlimited by Power by Anthony Robbins

To help you with leadership and business:

The 4 Dimensional Manager by Julie Straw; based on DiSC®

Constructive Conflict Management by John Crawley

The Discipline of Market Leaders by Michael Treacy & Fred Wiersema

The E Myth by Michael Gerber

The Five Dysfunctions of a Team by Patrick Lencioni

The Fred Factor by Mark Sanborn

Good to Great by Jim Collins

Leader Effectiveness Training by Thomas Gordon

Leadership 2.0 by Travis Bradberry and Jean Greaves

Leadership and the One Minute Manager by Ken Blanchard

Learning to Lead by Warren Bennis and Joan Goldsmith

The One Minute Manager Builds High Performance Teams by Ken Blanchard

The One Minute Manager by Ken Blanchard

Primal Leadership by Daniel Goleman

Principle Centered Leadership by Stephen Covey

ReWork by Jason Fried and Heinemeir Hansson

The Secret by Ken Blanchard & Mark Miller

See You at the Top by Zig Ziglar

The Social Styles Handbook: Find Your Comfort Zone and Make People Feel Comfortable with You by Larry Wilson

Speaking from the Gut by Jack Welch

The Weekly Coaching Conversation by Brian Souza

Winning by Jack Welch

Working with Emotional Intelligence by Daniel Goleman

To combat worry:

The Be (Happy) Attitudes by Robert Schuller

The Joy of Meditation by Jack and Cornelia Addington

The Power of Positive Thinking by Norman Vincent Peale

Stop Worrying and Start Living by Dale Carnegie

To help you with CHANGE:

Change Your Questions Change Your Life by Marilee Adams

Rising Strong by Brene Brown

Transitions by William Bridges

Who Moved My Cheese by Spencer Johnson

To learn to face fear:

Excuses BE Gone by Wayne Dyer

Feel the Fear and Do It Anyway by Susan Jeffers

Transform Your Life by Barbara King

These two are out of print, but if can find them, they are great:

Feel Free and *Risking* by David Viscott

To build self-esteem:

Codependent No More: How to Stop Controlling Others and Start Caring for

Yourself by Melody Beattie

I Declare by Joel Osteen

Life Strategies by Phil McGraw

Pulling Your Own Strings by Wayne Dyer

Self Matters by Phil McGraw

What You Think of Me Is None of My Business by Terry Cole Whitaker

When Perfect Isn't Good Enough by Martin Anthony & Richard Swinson

You Can Heal Your Life by Louis Hay

To build a positive attitude:

Aspire by Kevin Hall

Become a Better You by Joel Osteen

Change Your Thoughts, Change Your Life by Wayne Dyer

The Compound Effect by Darren Hardy

Cooked by Chef Jeff Henderson

If You Can See It You Can Be It by Chef Jeff Henderson

The Power of Positive Thinking by Norman Vincent Peale

The Secret book and DVD by Rhonda Byrne

Success Through A Positive Mental Attitude by W. Clement Stone and Napoleon Hill

What Happy People Know by Dan Baker

Your Best Life NOW by Joel Osteen

To help retrain your mind:

As A Man Thinketh by James Allen

Awaken the Giant Within by Anthony Robbins; any of his books or CDs

Change Your Mind Change Your Life by Brian Tracy – also his CD *Million Dollar Habits*

The Joy of Adulthood by Sylvia Sultenfuss

Living Deliberately by Harry Palmer and any AVATAR course www.avatarepc.com

Seeds of Greatness by Denis Waitley

Becoming a courageous woman:

Born to Lead by Bill Lamond

The Dance of the Dissident Daughter by Sue Monk Kidd

#Girlboss by Sophia Amoruso

Lean In by Sheryl Sandberg

When the Heart Waits by Sue Monk Kidd

A Woman's Worth by Marianne Williamson

To build your Assertiveness:

Constructive Conflict Management by John Crawley

Crucial Conversations by Patterson, Grenny, McMillan & Switzler

Crucial Confrontations by Patterson, Grenny, McMillan & Switzler

Fierce Conversations by Susan Scott

Unlimited Power by Anthony Robbins

To improve your relationships:

The Emotional Intelligence Quick Book by Travis Bradberry and Jean Greaves

How to Win Friends and Influence People by Dale Carnegie

The Personality Code by Travis Bradberry

To improve your spouse/significant other relationships:

5 Love Languages by Gary Chapman

Getting the Love You Want by Harville Hendrix

His Needs, Her Needs by Willard Harley

Keeping the Love You Find by Harville Hendrix

To conquer anger:

Change Your Brain Change Your Life by Dr. Daniel Amen

Pulling Your Own Strings by Wayne Dyer

You Can Heal Your Life by Louis Hay

To improve your health:

Eat Right for Your Blood Type by Dr. Peter J. D'Adamo

The New Atkins for a New You by Dr. Eric Westman, Dr. Stpehen Phinney, and Dr. Jeff Volek

The Virgin Diet by JJ Virgin

Younger Next Year by Chris Crowley and Dr. Henry Lodge

Younger Next Year for Women by Chris Crowley and Dr. Henry Lodge

www.ingramcontent.com/pod-product-compliance
Lightning Source LLC
Chambersburg PA
CBHW071458040426
42444CB00008B/1400